GUIDE
TO A
GREAT
CAREER

GUIDE TO A GREAT CAREER

Landing the **Dream Job**

OUSSOU KOUAME REMI

GUIDE TO A GREAT CAREER
LANDING THE DREAM JOB

Author Credits: Kouame Remi Oussou

New International Version (NIV)
Holy Bible, New International Version®, NIV® Copyright ©1973, 1978, 1984, 2011 by Biblica, Inc.® Used by permission. All rights reserved worldwide.

iUniverse books may be ordered through booksellers or by contacting:

iUniverse
1663 Liberty Drive
Bloomington, IN 47403
www.iuniverse.com
1-800-Authors (1-800-288-4677)

ISBN: 978-1-5320-7936-8 (sc)
ISBN: 978-1-5320-7937-5 (e)

Library of Congress Control Number: 2019911320

Print information available on the last page.

iUniverse rev. date: 08/06/2019

Do not worry of being unemployed;
worry you rather be worthy of a job.
— Confucius

To my children, Oussou Sarah Elielle and
Oussou Yao Ephraim Shalom

CONTENTS

FIGURES

WARNING

This guide emerged from two sets of experiences. For one, it originates in my experiences as a professor of sociology and anthropology at Alassane Ouattara University of Bouake (Ivory Coast), where, in addition to teaching, grading, and supervising students' research, I was coordinator of the task force named Cellule pour l'Emploi et l'Employabilite, which guides, orients, nurtures, coaches, mentors, and finds career- and skills-development opportunities for students. Second, it is the product of my experiences in counseling, workforce development, career development, and readiness as a work-based learning experience.

I was born and raised in Africa, but in my view the problems that constitute the backdrop of this guide hold a universal value, meaning that no matter where the job searcher comes from and whatever one's majors or skills may be, without a proper preparation, one may face the same difficulties in finding a job, particularly one's dream job.

ACKNOWLEDGMENTS

I need to give credit where credit is due by thanking those who contributed directly to bringing this book to life.

First of all, I would like to humbly thank the US government, along with the US people, for granting me the opportunity to live out one of my lifelong dreams of learning English—by way of immersion through the Hubert H. Humphrey Fellowship Program, which allowed me to spend ten months in the United States, specifically at Pennsylvania State University.

Second, I would like to wholeheartedly thank the whole staff of the Penn State Career Services, beginning with the director, Dr. Orndorff, and particularly Mr. Matthew William Ishler, my supervisor who tirelessly and selflessly contributed to my knowledge in two different ways, technically and linguistically. Each and every opportunity to shadow him provided me with the occasion to learn something new, whether it was technical knowledge on career advising and career development or new English words.

Third, my thanks go to Georges Henault, professor emeritus of the University of Ottawa, Canada, and president of the Conference Internationale des Dirigeants des Institutions d'Enseignement et de Recherche de Gestion d'Expression Francaise (CIDEGEF). I am highly indebted to him for his insightful comments and criticism.

Finally, I would like to thank all those who have indirectly played a part in the completion of this project.

INTRODUCTION

Unemployment is worldwide and touches mostly the youth. According to the International Labor Organization (ILO), the estimate number of unemployed was more than 192 million in 2018, and it is not expected to decrease. The total number of the unemployed is expected to reach 1.3 million per year with a projected rate of vulnerable employment set to rise to 17 million per year in 2018 and 2019.[1] In the past, a degree from a university was a likely way to secure a position, but it is no longer the case today, regardless of the type of career path. Even worse, some graduates are expected to cover a dozen careers throughout their working lives. Studies revealed that the less far the student goes in his studies, the higher his chances to receive employment over the short term.

There are also specific job market expectations depending on the level of the job market itself, the level of study, the type of training, and the nature of the disciplinary field. Coupled with specific worker categories and crowding the job market, that raises other concerns.[2]

Some of the direct consequences are the continuous increase in contingent workforce (underemployment, temporary and part-time contracts, informal work in developing and underdeveloped countries, etc.), spurring volatility, and poverty. The direct effect of that situation is the impossibility to invest in education in general and higher education

---

[1] International Labor Organization, *World Employment Social Outlook: Trends* (Geneva, ILO: 2018).
[2] These categories are the disabled, incarcerated and ex-offenders, immigrants, international students, LGBTQ, minorities, new workers and millennials, older customers, veterans, volunteers, women, workers in transition, teens, and young adults.

in particular—and thus the creation of a gap between the poor and the well-off.

Graduate unemployment is an entangled social fact. The explaining factors are as numerous as they are complex. At the root of the issue, three elements stand out, ranging from the refusal of the university to adapt to the changing nature of the economy in spite of the "massification" and the learning challenges that it poses to students, decrease or withdrawal of funding by governments, and the apathy of multinationals that prefer to hire midlevel skilled workers or resort to in-house training rather than invest in the training of graduate students at universities.

As a result, finding a job for a graduate is a pain in the neck, and so is the choice of a career path.

However, the possibility for the graduate student to create a sustainable life for himself is still out there. One of the foundations of higher education is to expose the student to think theoretically, critically, and creatively.

Furthermore, in the course of studies, both through classroom and extracurricular activities, the average student acquires technical knowledge related to one's major (hard skills), people skills (soft skills), and skills that one can use across various industries (transferable skills).

On the basis of the foregoing remarks, a student's academic skills remain strong tools for one to come up with innovative solutions either for the understanding and interpretation of companies' difficulties (and turning them into higher productivity and profit) or to spearhead the creation of job opportunities for oneself.

Why This Book, and Whom Is It For?

Do you want to become a go-getter and sought-after job seeker? Do you want to beat recruiters, hiring managers, human resource professionals, and HR representatives at their own game? Simply put, would you like to be successful in your career? Then this book is for you.

It is no secret that the job world is plagued with a number of issues. In a fast-paced world led by technology, education has a hard time keeping pace with a fickle labor market. Yet there exists a tremendous amount of available resources. Many books and articles have addressed the topic, some briefly and some extensively. Beside the growing number of books that have been written on the subject, including books on personal development, there are online tools, including social media, and on-site help through career counseling, coaching, and mentoring via career services.

The necessary conclusion is that the early career planning and preparation is flawed. The process has to be reversed, and planning a career has to be an exciting process instead of being a pain in the neck. No matter the occupation you want to enter, you need to consider your interests, how long you want to be in school, how much money you want to make, the type of work you want to do, the potential for job growth, and job trends in the specified industry.

On the other hand, we are all aware that most of the jobs we see today will vanish, and this occurrence will depend on how fast technology takes hold of the sector. Furthermore, the way job descriptions are phrased looks like hiring managers are looking for robots to perform the job. Often the responsibilities involved in the role are so highly pitched that it seems likely that they will not find anyone who can comply with all them. What's more, the job-description section generally finishes with statements such as "this list of duties and responsibilities is not intended to be an exhaustive list of all responsibilities, duties, and skills." In other cases, the hiring managers are so cynical as to write the following: "Duties, responsibilities, and activities may change at any time with or without notice." Sounds familiar, doesn't it? I am sure it does. Fortunately, in most cases, recruiters and other HR gatekeepers are forced to lower their expectations and settle for the second-best candidate on hand.

At the same time, there are successful people whose extraordinary career looks like a fairy tale, but what many do not know is the sum of the efforts these people have been putting into their lives to get to where they are.

It all comes down to good preparation beforehand. All college students can follow the same path and be successful. For once, wouldn't it be great to break the grip of recruiters and HR gatekeepers? Wouldn't it be good news to end the tyranny of recruiting managers by giving them a taste of their own medicine and beating them at their own game?

This practical guide aims at providing students with the proper preparation, planning, tools, resources, and guidance to make informed decisions about their career choices throughout their lifetime, which goes well beyond term papers and test grades. For the first time, the job seeker is in command, controls the entire process, and does not have to rely on the psychological moments of the employers. Job seekers are in the driver's seat because getting their dream jobs has never been so close. It is undeniably true that we all have a set of skills that we have been developing since childhood through our gifts, talents, education, interests, knowledge, and experiences, which we can use effectively and efficiently in various professional settings until we have reached the intentionality or self-reflection that will enable us to tap efficiently into these hidden strengths.

Unlike a book in the classical sense of the term, the merit of this practical guide, this vade mecum, divided into three main parts, lies at the intersection of career education and career readiness, drawing on the "Parachute Way" for job hunting. Its uniqueness is that it takes the prospective job hunter step-by-step from the preparation phase to the landing of one's dream job.

With this said, any higher education institution striving to attract and retain students, particularly with the aim to enrich students' overall experience on and outside of campus, may find it useful.

On a final note, this guide will instill in the job hunter a way of thinking and acting that goes far beyond the sheer career-building process to aim at a long-lasting impact on both one's personal and professional journey.

How to Use It

There are countless reasons why an applicant does not get past even the screening process and so is denied an interview. However, good background preparation helps. Nothing can be achieved without a proper preparation, which this book teaches step-by-step. Without that preparation, it is unlikely that the job seeker will land the job that suits his or her particular professional purpose.

Originally planned to be short, this book grew in size as it progressed, which is good news because I had the latitude to explore career exploration and career development leading theoretical frameworks in the field.

However, I strived to simplify complex tenets into simple, understandable principles to avoid overwhelming the reader. By so doing, I hope that if any merit whatsoever has to be granted to this book, I would like it to be its step-by-step approach to prepare the future job applicants for a successful transition to the workforce.

This book is primarily designed to accompany the student in one's career-preparation and job-search journey, but it can be used by any college student as an individualized career-development plan. One can use it on a day-to-day basis because it walks the prospective job applicant all the way from doubt to greatness on the job-search journey through practical and sensible tips. Those who are in a situation of career transition can use the book to remain employable.

The first part addresses the various factors to consider when making a career choice and setting career goals, including choice of major and acquisition of hard, soft, and transferable skill sets through trainings, internship, externship, job placement, and other available services and resources.

The second part covers the development of the common practical tools like résumés and cover letters, which are necessary to apply for job openings.

The third part deals with the broad entrepreneurship mind-set that the student is privileged to use, either by setting one's own business or by proposing a wide range of solutions to companies.

PART I

Career Preparation and Career Readiness

Breaking the Stronghold of the Employers

It is generally argued that there are fields that work, and there are those that lead naturally to unemployment either because they are saturated or there is no demand for them. I can hear parents telling their children to steer clear of certain sectors. I have a friend of mine who would have excelled as a painter because he has a lot of talent in drawing, but because of pressure from his family to choose a noble profession, he wound up studying law simply because a professional in the field of law is socially well thought of. Oftentimes our families push us into certain choices that can turn out to be counterproductive for us. The latest news I received from him is that he became an office clerk.

With this said, it is necessary to end the tyranny of employers. In a world that is controlled by a capitalist and profit-led economy, which has given the companies the power to hire and fire whom they want and when they want without being held accountable, nothing can be more misleading and further from the truth than the skill-mismatch rhetoric of employers. What really happens is that we live under the tyranny of recruiters who treat job seekers like vulgar beggars. They are inconsiderate of the hard work, skill sets, and experiences that they strive to bring to the table. The good news is that the economy grows and diversifies at the same time, and therefore labor demand will still exist. It is upon the prospective job seeker to void these kinds of narratives and fulfill his or her professional dream.

Why Is It Necessary to Plan One's Career Ahead?

In this day and age, it is necessary to plan ahead for one's career, and it is necessary to have a proactive attitude. Any leader or manager would recognize that an organization cannot function without setting a certain number of clear and specific objectives, based on available resources and activities. They must lay out the courses of action to take to efficiently and effectively achieve these goals. That is what they call in their jargon managing by objectives (MBO).[3]

Sparing the details of this management approach, I would like to outline that one of the main advantages of MBO is "planning for results instead of planning for work," highlighting the long-term process guided by clear goals.

In reality, planning encapsulates a number of sheer advantages, the first of them being that it offers a road map and a compass for the action. In addition, it constitutes a bulwark against uncertainty and allows one to take corrective action in time. In a nutshell, planning ahead avoids being caught off guard, providing a backup plan, particularly in job market that has become more and more unpredictable.

Then again, I am not talking of the rigid and compelling way of planning that managers and leaders are familiar with if they want their organizations to meet its goals. I am not requiring thinking right away of all the minutiae as the managers do. My point is that the job seeker must not wait till the last minute to begin thinking of one's career. I am probably taking the matter too seriously because one thing I am sure of is that each and every person since childhood has been planning. Whether thinking of the upcoming meeting with friends or the monthly budget, we all plan our on a daily basis.

This said, what is entailed in college students planning ahead for their careers? The current economic situation speaks for itself. In the face of massification in higher education, the number of graduates has

---

[3] The expression was coined by Peter F. Drucker in his seminal book *The Practice of Management* (New York: Harper & Row, 1954).

dramatically increased, tipping the scales in favor of demand. By so doing, more pressure has been put on students to possess at once the technical skills and knowledge acquired from formal learning institutions, as well as soft skills they are supposed to get through relevant job experiences. In that sense, early career exploration and preparation can set them apart and increase their chances of obtaining employment after high school or college.

Although the necessity to plan ahead may seem pointless at an early stage in life, author Shona Schmall compares the absence of planning to college students studying feverishly for their final exams, sometimes relying on doping products to boost the capacity of the brain. What happens at that time is simple: the brain may have powerful capacity for retention, but it cannot absorb so much knowledge in such a short amount of time. We all know what ensues in such situations: stress caused by fear of failure.

Planning your career will help you make the most of your time, resources, and energy each and every day. Don't think that planning your career and future goals is the same now as it was when you were in elementary school and your teacher asked you what you want to be when you grow up. While you might still want to be an astronaut or a firefighter, but achieving your dreams takes dedication and focused efforts, not just playing with your toy space shuttle or fire truck. If you are planning your career and future, here are some tips that will help you achieve everything you have always dreamed of.

Planning ahead gives plenty of time to refurbish one's professional project, pinpoint the risks, feel more in control, be confident, and have less stress. Furthermore, planning beforehand helps one to be more organized and focused on the types of job and organizations that better align with one's background experience. It also helps to identify the additional skills needs to better market oneself.

It should be stressed that planning is a key element of efficiency in life. The psychological benefits are tremendous. It keeps you focused, motivated, and self-confident enough to make more informed decisions about your life and get better results. In addition, it is a fact that many young people embark on studies without a global vision or real choice on their own, which sometimes leave them stranded.

Finally, during schooling it is often difficult to "lift the head from the handlebars" and project into the future, but planning one's career in advance has the tremendous advantage of building self-confidence and self-assertiveness. Most of all, it is one of the conditions for a successful and fulfilling life.

Age Matters When It Comes to Career Planning

Many analysts suggest that career exploration should begin at an early age. Here is the grim reality why it is necessary to begin contemplating one's future job. We all know now that in our fast-paced world, it is better to not wait until the last minute to plan one's career. However, an assumption that the youth still hold is that they have plenty of time ahead to deal with this kind of issue, so they do not need to rush to plan their career for the moment. Such an assumption may have proven right in the past, where thousands of jobs were out there waiting for takers, but things have gone the other way around, and they have even have gone sour for job hunters, particularly graduate students.

The right question to ask is "What is the right stage to begin planning one's career?" It is never too soon to get an idea of what one wants to be in the future.

In a scholarly article published in 2000 in the *Journal of Career Development*, Carolyn S. Magnuson of Lincoln University and Marion F. Starr of the Missouri Department of Elementary and Secondary Education drafted "How Early Is Too Early to Begin Life Career Planning?" They asked the paramount question: "How early is too early to begin thinking about what one wants to do with his or her life?" The next sentence reads, "We propose that it is never too early to consider ways to help children achieve self-fulfillment." That provides an insightful answer to the question.

To give a clear answer to the previous question, although career exploration and planning implicitly began in childhood, career decision and subsequent skills acquisition should begin at the high school level, or at college level at the latest. Based on the following information, any job hunter can land any job one wants provided one has good preparation.

The Appropriate Mental Attitude Counts

Getting ready for employment implies putting on the right mental attitude. The journey itself can turn out to be lengthy and unpredictable, with so many twists and turns that it takes a certain amount of determination and self-motivation to stick to the goal. With this said, self-motivation supersedes determination. To say it plainly, you have to discipline and motivate yourself. It is generally admitted that factors like family, friendship, time management, sleep, and teacher engagement, are critical to student success, but self-motivation and self-discipline account for at least half of these predictors. It is like learning a foreign language.

The Online Business Dictionary defines self-motivation as "the ability to do what needs to be done, without influence from other people or situations."[4] One thing you need to understand is that this drive will never come from other people. It comes from you and you alone.

Of course, other extrinsic factors like family members, friends, and network may contribute to your motivation, but not as much as yourself. It is your own responsibility to nurture these goals because they are yours alone, and the rewards (which include self-development and personal fulfillment) that derive from them will be yours. As such, you are the only one who is aware of the amount of endeavor you have to pull off to achieve them. In the process, the most difficult thing that might confront you is how to keep this motivation at a constant level. It is a matter of fact that keeping a high level of motivation over a period spanning career exploration and effective employment is easier said than done, but regardless of the difficulties and obstacles, you have to keep your eyes on why you set these goals, which is enough to keep you going.

On the other hand, self-discipline is another quality that a prospective job achiever has to factor in if one wants to reach his goals. It is defined as "the ability you have to control and motivate yourself, stay on track and do what is right."[5]

Something that deserves to be remembered is that at a point in one's studies, it is not only about intelligence but rather determination, a positive mind-set, courage, and resilience backed by self-discipline. These are the main keys to overall success.

---

[4] https://www.dictionary.com/browse/self-motivation.

[5] https://www.yourdictionary.com/self-discipline.

Commitment to a Lifelong Learning Attitude

Any student needs to understand that deciding to go to college is a vocation. Therefore one is in it for the long haul. Also known as constant learning or continuous learning, lifelong learning features the idea of always acquiring new knowledge, skills, and expertise, or upgrading and honing the old ones. One of its characteristics is the curious mind.

On a psychological level, continuous learning stimulates the brain cells. By so doing, it not only enhances the cognitive ability of the individual, including increased problem-solving ability and memory, but from a personal growth perspective, it also remains the best way to reexamine assumptions, values, methods, policies, and practices.

On a professional level, continuous learning is crucial for the development of knowledge and new competencies, leading to new skill sets and professional opportunities.

Constant learning is fully part and parcel of personal and professional development endeavor in an effort to avoid stagnation. On top of that, it is the only remedy to adjust to a fast-changing environment.

To live a life without continuous learning is so unthinkable that there are a number of sayings that center on the knowledge that does not stop evolving. For instance, "Time and tide wait for no man," "To stand still is to retreat," "Not to grow is to slide backward," "He who stops being better stops being good."

Similarly, and maybe here as a condemnation, the idea of losing existing skills when one fails to build upon them is illustrated in the Parable of the Talents. Before he set on a journey, a master entrusted his three slaves with a certain amount of money. Whereas the first two put the money to work at a certain rate, the third one dug a hole and buried it. Upon his arrival, the verdict of the master did not delay. He praised those who made a better use of their stewardships and severely blamed the one who stashed his share. "Therefore take the talent from him and give it to the one who has ten. For the one who has will be given more, and he will have more than enough. But the one who does not have, even what he has will be taken from him."[6]

---

[6] The Bible, King James Version (Oxford UP, 1998).

Taking all this into account, the simple truth portrayed here is the paramount importance of continuously and relentlessly building on what we already have with the risk of losing out it altogether.

Building the Career Capital: The Career Development Project

General Considerations

How do we choose a career in the first place? Some seem to have their future career paths already mapped out, whether from an innate ability or from their parents. Others have a hard time deciding what is best for them, mostly because they are still locked into the dilemma of what their heart longs for and what other people want them to become due to social status.

With the idea in mind, I do not want to rekindle the old debate about "do what you love" and "follow your passion," which are based on the saying "Choose a job you love, and you will never have to work a day in your life." That has become the common norm, with flexibility and adaptability, or even underemployment.[7]

I am not saying that it is a bad idea to follow your passion, but at the same time, it is necessary to weigh the constantly changing working environment and prepare for it in advance. That's good for you if both coincide, but what should matter in either case is to add value to what you do. In other words, how can you do your very best no matter what the circumstances are? That is the bottom line.

Career Planning Steps

Planning for a future career may seem boring due the fact that it can be time-consuming, but the effort is worth it because it will save you worries in the future. Some may call it a career plan, others will term it a career action plan, and still others name it a personal and professional project. Whatever

---

[7] Of an unknown origin, this adage is attributed by some attribute to Confucius (551 BC, in the district of Zou Province du Shandong near present-day Qufu, China), whereas others attribute it to Arthur Szathmary (1916–2013), a member of the Philosophy Department at Princeton University from 1947 to 1986.

its name may be, the job seeker needs an action plan for one's future career. That is when the professional project comes into play.

The phrase embodies the notion of an objective to attain and a strategy to put in place, including resources to look for. In other words, a professional project means to "set a clear and precise goal of research around a specific profession, in a specific sector of activity, in a precise geographical area." It designs with a certain amount of details the career plan. It is important because it is like the blueprint of an effective job search strategy in the way that it helps the job searcher align one's own aspirations with the opportunities that are available or likely to be created on the job market by weighing one's means and resources.

The main benefit associated with having a professional project before confronting the job market is that it helps job seekers take stock of the skills they already possess, the ones they do not have, and the ones they need to work toward to acquire.

This said, a number of theorists have given a lot of thought on the matter. John Holland with his five-pronged underlying frameworks, Lent Brown and Hackett, Frank Parsons—all these thinkers view career development as a series of sequences giving deep insights into the various steps that have to be followed for effective career development.

Yet the professional project mentioned in this guide, as a self-marketing tool, does not have to be considered a set of linear actions. On the contrary, it can take twists and turns till the end goal is reached. It is also worth mentioning that the career planning road map can be modified at any time to adjust to new developments.

On the other hand, it is worth mentioning that the ultimate goal of this exercise is to help the prospective job seeker develop a number of skills, which include decision-making and self-reliance. Theorists define four major steps combining one's skills: capabilities, the trends in the market, training and education, and implementation. These substantially boil down to two aspects: self-knowledge and market assessment.

Self-Knowledge

Like a writing piece, it has to begin somewhere and also end somewhere. The first step to achieving an effective and impactful professional project is self-knowledge. The Online Cambridge Dictionary defines self-knowledge as an understanding of oneself and one's own abilities. In concrete terms, self-knowledge encompasses not only the individual's abilities, talents, gift, values, skills, knowledge, experience, and strengths but also one's interests, dreams, motivations, ambitions, and passions. In this sense, it is close to self-awareness. An old aphorism says, "Know thyself." Down the road of the journey of discovery of one's identity, being aware of one's own value and what ticks puts you on the path to deciding the right set of steps and actions to take.

But self-knowledge goes beyond taking stock of the positive side of yourself. It also has to take into account limitations, because it is so easy to be mistaken about qualities one does not have. Indeed, our narcissist and egoistic nature incline us to believe that we are more important than we really are.

Instead, the wise Buddha acknowledges, "There are those who lament their foolishness, but this already is not foolishness; more foolish is someone who calls himself intelligent without knowing himself." It is more common than one may think, but we tend to be lenient when judging ourselves, and we indulge in some qualities. Conversely, we may underestimate ourselves out of modesty, whereas there are virtues that we possess but ignore.

In the process, some introspective questions deem essential. As a matter of fact, a number of questions beg asking. "What am I good at? What do I like doing? What are my values? What are my weak spots? How can I improve them to stand out? What are my resources, including personal, familial, and social?" These are unavoidable questions. Finding answers to these questions helps you have a clear, compelling idea of what your career road map may be.

In addition, it may be helpful to call on family members and friends to assist you mapping your qualities and imperfections.

The professional project is the guiding thread of a future career. It allows you to orient yourself and make the right decisions step-by-step throughout your professional life.

Therefore the stage of the assessment has to take into account what you think are your strengths and weaknesses. The exercise is essential because once you reckon your worth and acknowledge your limitations, you may gradually work toward them to improve them over time. You may also shed what you might have in excess that is not necessarily good.

Career Pathways Exploration

Career Exploration Tools

After going through the self-consciousness process, it is time to scratch around for the prospective opportunities that the labor market has to offer. Beforehand, though, you have to consider what ticks the boxes you in your life. What would make you happy? A job that pays top dollar or something that offers good perspectives in terms of career? At the end of day, it all about what you consider as success and achievement. You may consider the possibilities offered by certain sectors of activity, trades, professions, or functions that may align with your current interests and future ambitions, particularly because you do not want to waste money, energy, and time on a sector that will not meet your basic requirements. For instance, after thorough self-analysis, you happen to understand that deep down, you are not for mathematics, and you find figures and calculations tedious and boring. You may not consider going into a career whose basics deal with figures, like accountancy. That's where honestly acknowledging your own limitations comes into play. In case you still have doubts about the career pathways you have been exploring,

I recommend you using a career assessment tool. I would not like to expand on Holland's career clusters and career codes, though, because at the end of the assessment, there is a thorough account of all the possibilities along with the underpinning theories. Indeed, according to Whiston and Rahardja, career assessment tools are applications that are meant to assist individuals see what types of careers are likely to fit them in accordance with their personalities (2005). Based on a series of questions determining attributes like data values, preferences, motivations, aptitudes, and skills, the results of the assessment provide the test taker with a cluster of occupations and professions that best suit their personalities. Drawing upon Holland's Code Personality Types, the assumption that lies behind them is that people are likely to thrive in a job setting that corresponds to their personality type.[8]

---

[8] For reference and further exploration, there are well-known and reliable career assessment tools available on the internet, some of them being chargeable like Myers-Briggs Type Indicator, Keirsey Temperament Sorter, Myplan.com, Big Five, 16 Personalities, iSeek "Clusters," MyNextMove, Mapp Test, Holland Code, and PI Behavioral Assessment. Most are available for free.

Designed to highlight candidates' possible strengths and limitations, these tools can be helpful in providing candidates with a wide variety of career options in the career exploration, career planning, and self-exploration process (Prince et al. 2003). In addition to that, their unique strengths and originality reside in the insight that the individuals might not have had prior to taking the assessment.

However, like any other assessment tool, the results of the tests may display results that do not match any of the core interests of the candidate at all. The way the questions are phrased or the available options for the answers are so wide apart that someone may fall into any of the proposed categories, and then one is forced to choose an answer that does not reflect one's choice, which may skew the data and end results. Another gap these tools may hide is their tendency to box test takers in career and skills categories. Interpretation of the results sometimes seems too tricky, and a candidate may require the assistance of a seasoned career counselor. Anyway, it is important to know what we are good at and what we need to improve upon to be competitive in the workplace.

Then again, this tool can offer only insights. It cannot overtake the individual's decision-making skills.

Career Decision

This step allows you to learn more about the nitty-gritty involved in each occupation that turns you on, which includes job roles, responsibilities, career prospects, salary range, and trade sustainability.

At this point, if you not want to be trapped in a profession that might not be in demand in the future, it is necessary to require experts' opinions. In other words, you need to consider career outlook, because it is obvious that some occupations we see today might not attract employers' attention and might not be around in ten or twenty years. After reflecting on the professional options, one must take into account the general trends of the world of work. The labor market is characterized by a state of permanent change, and it is necessary to consider long-term changes in the professions to observe the underlying trends that modify the structure of employment.

In this quest, the Bureau of Labor Statistics (BLS) might be an invaluable source of information. Its assessment about the trends of the employment rate for hundreds of occupations is updated every two years in the *Occupational Outlook Handbook*, which may guide your career path.

According to BLS, job outlook is "a statement that conveys the projected rate of growth or decline in employment in an occupation over the next 10 years; also compares the projected growth rate with that projected for all other occupations."[9]

The internet may prove a good entry point, along with libraries as available resource. In addition to that, you may want to consider asking for advice from some practitioners in the fields of your interests. They may provide you with insightful information about certain details that books will never show. And who knows? You might end up signing a contract, which may grow into a mentorship.

At this point in time, you may not have a clear picture of whatever resources you will mobilize later, but at the same time, your professional hunger should not lead you to consider things that could be well out of range because at the end of the day, your achievements hinge upon the availability of your resources.

After casting a wide net for a broad career search, it is necessary to reduce the search to a couple of professions that share some commonalities and have open options, or related fields of expertise. You do not want to stretch yourself too thin; the bottom line is being able to create a relevant tread of continuity for one's career that strengthens your employability portfolio.

Then again, it is worth mentioning that this guide is not a cookbook with ready-made recipes, but at least you have the right insight that will allow you to make informed decisions and act in a responsible fashion.

The Skills That Need to Be Developed or Strengthened

Now that you are equipped with a fairly good knowledge of the industry and professions that suit your ambition and interests, it is time to build up your knowledge capital by choosing the curricula that will help you build the necessary skills, knowledge, and experiences to achieve your professional goals. In a nutshell, it is time to build your career capital.

---

[9] https://www.bls.gov.

At this point in time, keep in mind that with any move you have to take, you need to stick to plan. This means that either extracurricular activities or coursework must share a common point, contributing to building skills, knowledge, and experiences for the job you want. Education provided in learning settings is made up of two main sets of abilities: hard skills and soft skills.

Hard Skills versus Soft Skills

In essence, hard skills are the technical skills necessary to perform the type of job for which training has been conducted. They are types of knowledge and abilities taught and learned in formal classroom settings as part of education and training programs, which include college, apprenticeships, short-term training classes, online courses, certification programs, and on-the-job training. They are characterized by their specificity to subject matter or course content like typing, writing, math, reading, programming, and accountancy. In this sense, they are called functional competencies because they are job specific. They can be measured and are generally sanctioned by a diploma or certificate. One of their highlights is that they can be pinpointed because they act as a metric for a certain level of competency to fit in a position. That is why it is easy for employers to list them in job descriptions, and so they are expected to find them in applicants' cover letters and résumés. The Applicant Tracking Systems (ATS), the "type of software used by companies to assist with human resources, recruitment, and hiring processes," is a relevant example of how hard skills can be measured and traced. The point here is that the algorithm of these machines is based on the search for key specific words related to a number of skills and titles involved in the advertised position.

No matter an ATS may select your résumé based on the multiple combinations of skills and titles you may have included in your application, the bottom line is that you need to be really good at what you are supposed to be doing, meaning that any subject or content you learned should be at your fingertips.

Unfortunately, most students lure themselves into the mistaken idea that once they graduate and find an employment, they are done with learning. You need to understand that learning is a lifelong project that ends in the grave.

Whereas hard skills refer to the expertise acquired through formal education and training programs that enable an individual to fulfill the requirements associated with a specific professional role, soft skills feature the abilities of an individual to get along with the others. They inform how one relates to one's fellow human being. That is the reason why they are often called interpersonal skills or people skills. They would include, but are not limited to, personality traits and values like communication skills, listening skills, leadership, empathy, and teamwork. The difference between both types of skills is that hard skills are quantifiable and taught in formal training settings, whereas soft skills are noncognitive and nonmeasurable skills. Because we are not taught soft skills in any formal training setting, we acquire and develop them over the course of our lives through education and experiences. It stands to reason that we are all endowed with some of these skills, but some are fully fledged and noticeable whereas others are still bubbling. In most cases, we are hardly aware that we possess these skills, and therefore we need someone to raise our awareness of them.

Oftentimes employers complain that training graduates is inappropriate for the employment market due to their lack of on-the-job experience. What employers ignore most of the time is that the class activities imparted to students contribute to building a number of skill sets. Maybe this misrepresentation does not necessarily lie with the employers because students themselves are ignorant of these skills.

In short, you have to develop both hard and soft skills, which your study courses will equip you with provided that you are aware of them.

Let us take the examples of group projects, class presentations, and class assignments given to students. Has anyone ever thought of the goal of such tasks? What generally happens is students dodge these assignments and wait till the last moments to cram before the finals. On the surface, these activities seem trivial, and so are students' attitudes toward them. But in reality, it is obvious that these class activities represent the bulk of the soft skills—teamwork, communication skills, critical and analytical thinking—that employers praise in job descriptions, meaning that these various tasks need to be taken earnestly because they are not just single-day exercises. They are meant to teach students long-lasting skills. Robles defines them as "interpersonal qualities and personal attributes that one possesses" (Robles 2012), but I would call them social and life skills.[10] Much of the concern about this type of skill set is that, as highlighted earlier, their very nature does not make them accessible in a school or college environment, or through books, except for "trial and error" situations. This said, it has been suggested more and more that students should be involved in extracurricular activities and roles as a way to gain learning experiences outside the classroom. As a matter of fact, providing information in résumés or cover letters about how good one is at leading and communicating with others does not necessarily prove that one has leadership and communication skills. This is when a certain types of activity such as internships, part-time or summer employment, and volunteer or community work prove important.

However, in retrospect, deep down I remain convinced that we all have something to contribute in any interview situation; we simply have to know how to put it to use.

Preparing for a Backup Plan

In a constantly moving world and a skill-based economy, it is commendable to acquire other skill sets, the so-called transferable skills that are paramount to the workplace. The Online Business Dictionary apprehends these kinds of skills as "the aptitude and knowledge acquired through personal experience such as schooling, jobs, classes, hobbies, sports, etc."[11] Another online dictionary, the Cambridge Dictionary, defines it as, "Skills used in one job or career that can also be used in another."[12]

These are pretty much overlapping skills, and they are related to "any talent developed and able to be used in future employment." Their unique feature is that their usefulness spans different roles, and they can be used across various occupations.

Best-selling job-hunting author Richard Nelson Bolles, in his life-shaping book *What Color Is Your Parachute? A Practical Manual for*

---

[10] Marcel M. Robles, "Executive Perceptions of the Top 10 Soft Skills Needed in Today's Workplace," *Business Communication Quarterly* 75, no. 4 (2012): 453–465.

[11] http://www.businessdictionary.com/transferable-skills.html.

[12] https://dictionary.cambridge.org/dictionary/english/transferable-skills.

Job-Hunters and Career-Changers, viewed life as a series of experiences we all make in the course of our lives that can be transferred into the workplace.[13]

Probably based on his own life as an embedded Christian and a public speaker, Bolles divides these skills into three features: people skills (communicating, teaching, coaching, and supervising), data skills (record keeping, researching, translating, and compiling data), and things skills (operating computers/equipment, assembling, and repairing).

In today's fast-paced economy driven mostly by technology and globalization, some specific skills such as leadership and interpersonal communication are critical, as is technology savvy in the workplace.

Increasingly, regardless of the type of competencies sought after in a role, sentences like, "Strong working knowledge of Word, Excel, PowerPoint, Adobe Acrobat" or "Bilingual preferred" are extremely common in job descriptions, meaning that the more foreign languages you can have working knowledge in, the more opportunities you will access in your job quest.

It is worth mentioning, however, that although those skills can easily be acquired through community, church, and club activities, it is a horse of a different color for languages because learning foreign languages is related to one's life and professional goals. Most programs in college will propose one or two foreign languages to choose as part of the coursework, but it is up to those who want to enhance their chances of landing a better job to go the extra mile and learn one or two foreign languages. Needless to say, becoming a globally minded citizen requires time and dedication, but it ultimately pays off one way or the other.

Let us assume that at this stage of the career preparation, the student has done exercises through self-awareness; had explored the various career pathways based upon interests, motivation, resources, and market trends; has acquired both sufficient hard skills and soft and transferable skills; and is ready to enter the workforce.

---

[13] Richard N. Bolles, *What Color Is Your Parachute? A Practical Manual for Job-Hunters and Career-Changers*, Kindle Edition.

Looking for and Taking Advantage of
Existing Training or Career Resources

The higher rate of unemployment among graduate students has cast serious doubt over the efficiency of higher education across the world in terms of learning outcomes. As a result, career services have gradually emerged as significant interfaces that assist and support college students through various policies, initiatives, and activities with the ultimate goal to lead them to exciting and successful experiences both on and off campus. Some analysts go as far as to purport that the career services are among the important services on campus.

In essence, career services or career centers are offices that assist and support students and alumni in career preparation, career exploration, and counseling in order for them to make informed career decisions and transition from one career to another.

Most of colleges and universities today are fortunate enough to be equipped with career centers offices whose core responsibility is to help students get the most from their training on campus and prepare them for successful careers through extracurricular involvement.

Under these circumstances, they serve as interfaces between the students and the labor market. The career counselors and advisers have become critical to students' positive experiences on campus and after campus. Indeed, through walk-in sessions for résumé and cover letter fixing, internships finding, career fairs, mock interviews sessions, extra training, and workshops, these career centers contribute to the students' academic and personal growth and the development of job search skills relevant to the workforce.

Above and beyond this day-to-day duty, the career services remain vital in connecting students with alumni and companies, reinforcing the link between education and business, fostering entrepreneurship, and facilitating the transition from education to the world of work, all of which contribute to student success in a more competitive job market.

Although career services have a hard time reaching out to grab students' attention and get them to take advantage of the immense resources, career services remain the appropriate career and workforce development with resources to decipher career tests and assessments results. The key test results are often so intricate that the need of experts is required and highly recommended.

Extracurricular Learning Opportunities

In preparation for careering, extracurricular activities or engagement in order to get real world experiences are critical. Internships, externships, and volunteering are other ways to gain these experiences, in addition to increasing one's knowledge and skills.

As a rule of thumb, an internship is a period during which someone, generally a student, performs work for a company or organization with the aim of gaining work experience in a specific field related to one's studies. In some cases, the trainee can be paid. One thing that is paramount to remember about internships is that they can bridge the gap between academic and professional experience

When comparing internships and externships, a few differences appear. An externship is "a temporary training program in a workplace, especially one offered to students as part of a course of study." Typically, an externship is meant to last anywhere from a single day to eight weeks, compared to internships that are approximately eight weeks long. In addition to that, one of the other differences between internships and externships is that internships are often paid, or at least some small expenses like commuting are covered, and students get academic credit for their experience; externships are undertaken without any payment.

In an externship, the students are certainly physically present in the workplace, so the name *externship* might be a misnomer, but they shadow the professional or group of professionals they have been assigned to instead of being entrusted with real work responsibilities.

All things considered, externship does not truly compare with internship, but it still is an entry point to gaining hands-on work and professional experience, so do not be picky; it is good to grab them when they arise. Remember an externship allows you to observe the professionals in your field practicing their profession *in* situ, and it is an invaluable opportunity that can get your foot in the door with the networking opportunity that it offers.

Of course, an intern should not expect to accomplish rewarding tasks during the period of one's internship. It may happen that interns are jacks of all trades. In the worst-case scenarios, they are the people who do the menial tasks such as making coffee or running errands for supervisors.

On the surface, however, these pieces of work, as insignificant and devoid of meaning as they appear, are also fully part of the learning experience. How can you be entrusted with great things if you do not even know how to do the small ones? That is what the whole question is about. It all comes to how to make the most of your internship. In any events, the best bet to have a return on investment for the intern is to be fully engaged. This way, even though an offer is not made to you, at least you will leave an extremely positive image, and with some networking you might end up being recommended for a full-time position.

Another way to gain exposure and experience in the field is to get involved in community activities as a volunteer. It is excellent way to gain practical experiences either for one-day events or within organizations. Sometimes it is overwhelming for students to juggle their various assignments and extracurricular activities, but putting oneself at the service of others without pay benefits the volunteer in multiple ways. Indeed, beyond its psychological and humanistic values of well-being, self-confidence, self-esteem, and self-worth, giving oneself away to those who need assistance is an opportunity to develop new skills and broaden or hone those skill sets that already exist, such as interpersonal skills social skills and networking with experts in the fields of interest. Ultimately, that looks good on a résumé and gives the candidate a leg up on the competition.[14]

On top of that, it would be icing on the cake if you add to these already acquired skills broad experiences as a way to expose you to meaningful cultural diversity awareness.

Takeaways

Rising tuition and student debt coupled with graduates' rising unemployment rate continues to animate the debate about the need for higher education. The career mismatch will certainly increase in the future, and the imbalance between demand and supply may increase exponentially as never before, but the best candidates will always come out on top. Until

---

[14] For teenagers reaching the "fifth stage of identity vs. role confusion," highlighted by Erick Erickson, volunteering can help build "a sense of self and personal identity, through an intense exploration of personal values, beliefs, and goals."

a *modus vivendi* is found—if it's ever be found—it is necessary to protect yourself against what is known as the crisis of higher education.

All in all, one way to make the most of one's college years is to prepare for one's career. The pages above indicate the main steps for it. Acquisition of knowledge in college is important, but it has to be balanced with outside-the-classroom experiences like engagement in community activities, internships, and volunteering. All of them remain proven ways to get knowledge, experience, and networking.

However, all I have just said would be of no value at all if it were not supported by constant and hard work, discipline, and commitment. Studying hard means that the student must not only master the contents of the coursework but also do some research on his own, because it frequently happens that the instructor imparts probably only 40 percent of what the student should know. In addition to that, he must read all that comes to hand. Sometimes, excessive specialization prevents one from viewing the big picture. No matter which field you will be graduating in—engineering, liberal or fine arts, law, or economics—you will have to adopt an eclectic attitude toward learning. The secret to keep afloat in any field is continuous learning. In other words, be a proactive learner. Qualities like analytical skills and critical thinking are valued in the workplace, but they are acquired overnight; rather, they have to be sought after, nurtured, and groomed. The good news is that the more you learn, the more these intellectual qualities tend to naturally take place.

PART II

Developing a Job-Search Strategy

Assuming that you have followed the preparation phase of the career readiness process step-by-step and have built your career capital, you need now to step out to put in practice your knowledge, skills, and experiences.

But first and foremost, you need to put in place an action plan, which includes crafting a résumé and cover letter, effective networking, and getting ready for the interview.

Developing Common Jobs-Search Tools

The first practical tools that need to be developed are the résumé and the cover letter.[15]

Résumé Basics

The first element that needs to be crafted is the résumé. By all accounts, the résumé is the first contact point with the hiring manager in the job

---

[15] I am tempted to offer networking here as a job search tool, pretty much as résumé and cover letter, but networking is so pervasive through the whole process that it is difficult to suggest an exact moment when to apply or exert it. Our whole lives are networking opportunities.

application process. A résumé is a self-written document of one to two pages that compiles education, qualifications, personal interests, and previous work experiences when available. Expressed this way, it does not clearly show what it means for a layman.

Although there is a difference between the résumé and its counterpart, the curriculum vitae, let us see what the curriculum vitae, which has a Latin origin, has to say.[16]

According Merriam-Webster's online dictionary, the word *curriculum* means in New Latin "a course of study." Yet it originates in classical Latin and means "running" or "course" (as in "race course"). In this regard, it is close to the words like *corridor, courier,* and *currency,* and all of them derive from Latin *currere,* meaning "to run" because it shares indeed the same root with them.

In most occurrences, it is associated with *vitae,* which means life in Latin. Thus, a curriculum vitae, Latin for "course of (one's) life or career," is "a short account of one's career and qualifications prepared typically by an applicant for a position."[17]

Whether a résumé or a curriculum vitae, I cannot stress enough that they are marketing tools that are essential pieces of the hiring process. It is the first element that the hiring manager will come into contact with upon reception of the application package, and it helps him assess the skills of the applicant against the minimum job requirements, at least for short-listing purposes.

---

[16] Although both types of documents provide information about education, work experiences, and skills, the differences between résumé and CV lie in the length of the document and the background of the applicant. For instance, résumés for an entry-level position are crafted in one page, whereas CVs for the same level tend to be longer—say, two to three pages. CVs are meant for researchers and academics who need to display their teaching experience, degrees, research, awards, publications, presentations, and other achievements. Most résumés in the United States are competency based: they are personal marketing documents intended to showcase the candidate's skills, notable achievements, and work experience to the greatest advantage. US CVs, submitted for jobs in academia, scientific research, and medical fields, are credential based, providing a comprehensive (and often lengthy) listing of one's education, certifications, research experience, and professional affiliations and memberships.

[17] https://www.merriam-webster.com/dictionary/curriculum%20vitae

It means that this document needs to carry a very good first impression because more than just a mere application document, the résumé is actually a marketing tool. Similar to a manufactured product or service that is going into the market, it is a powerful way to brand your unique traits and accomplishments for a specific role. Let us be clear here, though. Crafting a résumé in no way means that the job is already under the belt, but at the very least, it should push the hiring manager to move forward and invite the applicant for an interview because the primary purpose of the résumé is, first and foremost, an interview. What does it mean in reality? It means that enough time and effort needs to be invested into its compilation. Do you have any idea of the number of applicants who are vying for the same job you applied to? Certainly not. The facts speak for themselves. According to *Forbes* magazine, "The average number of people who apply for any given job: 118 … Twenty-percent of those applicants get an interview … Many companies use talent-management software to screen resumes, weeding out up to 50% of applications before anyone ever looks at a resume or cover letter."[18] Another source states that the average number of applicants for a job opening is 250 and among those applicants only 2 percent will be shortlisted for an interview.[19]

As a consequence of this workload, a study found out that recruiters do not spend more than six seconds screening a résumé. It stands to mind that a dull and "tasteless" résumé will attract even less attention.

Given these dreadful facts, the need for a career preparation plan deems necessary, and the preparation of a résumé can stand out.

Résumés as marketing tools generally come in three formats: chronological, functional, and a combination of both. Before rushing into any of the types, it is best to pause and think about the type that suits better your personal work history. For an early career candidate without any significant work experience, the functional format better suits the purpose. With a work history, the chronological type is appropriate. Anyway, here are the highlights of the three formats and their characteristics.

---

[18] https://www.forbes.com/sites/jacquelynsmith/2013/04/17/7-things-you-probably-didnt-know-about-your-job-search/#68621dc43811.

[19] https://www.ebiinc.com/resources/blog/hiring-statistics.

Chronological-Format Résumé

It might be easier to change a job or find one for someone who has substantive previous work experience. In this case, the chronological résumé best suits this purpose. The chronological résumé describes the work history backward, from the most recent to older work. Ideally, it makes an inventory of all the work performed based on the most recent date to the least recent. It is probably one the most common types of résumés used by job seekers because it showcases work experience and puts forth the career progression, which can be spotted right away by hiring professionals.

As for its heading content, it lists an objective or career summary at the top, immediately followed by the different work experiences and the various skills acquired; education, certifications, and special skills come afterward.

Its focus is on work experience, so this résumé format is suitable for those who have already built up a solid work history in their fields.

Functional-Type Résumé

In spite of its popularity, the chronological résumé is not always a good match for all applications. In cases of applicants who are early in their career, those switching careers, or those having gaps in their work history, they need to showcase their skills and abilities (probably gained through internships and community activities). In this case, the functional résumé is the most adapted. A functional résumé, as its name indicates, is a résumé that focuses on functional areas, experiences, and specific skills that are related to a field of expertise. It is certainly less common than the chronological one, but it is said to be preferred by employers because it underscores the unique skills and capabilities that the candidate is offering. Ideally, it is used by those whose background work experience is not directly related to the position at hand but who have capitalized on their various soft and transferable skills acquired over college years, internships, and community involvement.

Its content should include a summary highlighting the skills that match the job description as a way to show right away to the employer that one meets the skills requirements to perform the job. The main part is essentially made of specific headings describing the key skills and qualifications by using keywords picked from the job description as titles for subheadings, describing with further detail role, responsibilities, and accomplishments. Along the way, the candidate should consider including in the résumé relevant projects (either personal or professional), putting an emphasis on complexities, success points, challenges, and how those challenges were addressed. Needless to say, the skills and capabilities mentioned in the thematic headings need to match the competencies described in the job requirements.

Nonetheless, no matter where the employment history stands, it has to be squeezed in at the end of the résumé. One of the specificities of this résumé format is that it should be accompanied by an extremely effective cover letter by insisting on your skills, experiences, and abilities that align with the most significant requirements listed in the position so as to balance the lack of work experience.

The functional résumé is probably the most complex résumé to write, but the effort and time put into designing and writing it is worth it.

The Combination-Style Résumé

The hybrid type résumé first highlights the skills and experience, followed by the documentation of work history. It is divided into two separate parts. The first part is similar to a functional résumé. The second one depicts the timeline of work experience. Indeed, like the functional résumé, the first part sketches key skills and capabilities of the applicant under the heading "qualifications summary." The second part "supports this introductory section with an account of prior work experience."

Although it is meant to "emphasize their skills over their work history, perhaps because they've changed career fields and much of their job history no longer reflects the skills they've gained that are appropriate for their new job targets," putting the skills and the work experience one after the other offers an opportunity to show one's unique value to the employer through the combination of strong skills and work history.

On the other hand, dividing the employment history into "Related Work Experience" and "Additional Professional Experience" is a good way to "focus your reader's attention on your most relevant experience while at the same time providing a complete work history."

Résumé-Writing Leads

After setting the table with the formats of the résumé, let us get down to the business of actually compiling a résumé. It is deplorable that employers think that a piece of paper can contain all the skills with which an individual is endowed. Anyway, one better way to go about crafting it is to first decide on the right format. Second, once the appropriate style is decided on, it is necessary to start brainstorming qualifications, experience, and achievements.

A résumé, as previously mentioned, is a bundle of information that proves that the applicant is worth considering for the advertised position. That said, there are elements that are optional, including career objective or a picture. However, it is a different story for the skills, education, and work history sections, which are considered to be the core information of the document.

In this day and age, with the spread of technology, multiple sites provide applicants with résumé formats, and some of them are well made. In any case, a thorough list of all the achievements, skills, and education (and their dates) need to be listed, with an emphasis on the accomplishments because at the end of the day, the relevancy and effectiveness of the résumé will be assessed against the job profile. It is better to be time efficient by choosing a format and fill it in with your skills, credentials, and education instead of designing a résumé from scratch. It is advised to use action verbs to describe work experience.

The next step you need to take is to make your résumé sound professional by keeping it as clear and simple as possible, proofreading it, and addressing as much as possible the opening requirements.

At this stage of the process, you may consider seeking the advice of a career adviser who may help in editing and catching typos. Of course, it is not advisable to go without an interim version you have drafted yourself. It shows how committed you are yourself to your goals.

One thing that you need to keep in mind in putting the last touches to your résumé is that it will first be scanned by an ATS before a human gets the chance to glance at it. Like any machine, the ATS is programmed to spot the right words highlighted in the job description, which means that you have to be careful in the selection of the relevant keywords, skills, and abilities that match the job requirements.

Once the résumé gets pass the ATS, it will land on the desk of the hiring manager. As human beings, managers are moved by emotions, and most important their minds are blown by facts, so you need to elicit these feelings in them. Why not use what advertising and marketing specialists do best? You need to use the persuasive power of positive emotions to engage them to look favorably upon your résumé. In practical terms, you need to highlight and emphasize the accomplishments in a specific and powerful manner.

Last but not least, it should be remembered that it is absolutely out the question to have just one copy of the résumé to circulate for any application, even if it is in the same field, much less with multiple openings at the same company or organization. By so doing, it conveys the idea of laziness, sloppiness, and lack of originality. Who would like to work with such individuals?

A sample of the three types of résumé can be found in the appendix of this book, but it is only for reference purposes because a résumé is not a one-size-fits-all document, it needs to be modified and constantly updated to suit the job requirements.

A résumé is typically sent with a cover letter, and as its name indicates, it is a document that provides additional information on your skills and experiences in the form of a letter.

Cover Letter

How many of job seekers are you aware of? How many seconds do employers spend scanning a cover letter? Based on statistics, it's three seconds at most. This is one more reason you must write an outstanding cover letter.

The cover letter, like the résumé, is a self-marketing tool that employers use to scour suitable applicants for interview. For this reason, before even trying to put pen to paper to jot down the first words of a cover letter, you need to understand what the cover letter is, what it intends to do, and what it covers. You need to fully understand what the employer is looking for. Generally, a cover letter is apprehended as a letter sent with a résumé to explain the reason why someone is applying for an advertised position by an organization. It is equally called a covering letter, motivation letter, motivational letter, and letter of motivation.[20] It is recommended to keep it on one page, although some may take only the half of the page. One of my female friends told me a story about a lady applicant who, as a cover letter for a job listing, simply wrote something like "If you do not hire me immediately, someone else will do it." The hiring manager was so intrigued that he invited the lady for an interview. Unfortunately, at the time the manager checked in, another offer was already made to the lady. This might come as an extreme example, but it illustrates how tricky looking for a job can be.

Cover letters come in four different types. Depending on the applicant's circumstances and the job requirements, there is the cover letter when the candidate has no work experience, the cover letter with some work experience, the cover letter that requires no résumé, and the cover letter for an unadvertised position. Regardless of the type chosen to apply for the position, its purpose is to state how the applicant's relevant skills and experiences are a good fit for the job description. In other words, the full understanding of the job description is the key to drafting a cover letter that spotlights the candidate's best personal and professional attributes. The secret to writing an effective cover letter is to tailor it to the required qualifications in the best possible way. In other words, the application needs to pay close attention to the specifics highlighted in the advertisement. It is highly recommended to do so not for its own sake but to get past the ATS. For instance, if the job description includes a series of essential skills and experiences, as well as desirable skills, all of them need to be addressed one by one. It is argued that the applicant who fails to address the required qualifications in a specific and precise way is automatically rejected.

Besides, it is not enough that the substance of the cover letter shows how it matches the needs of the job description; it also needs to be original and creative.

As a rule of thumb, a well-crafted cover letter that begins with catchy words entices the hiring manager to read it. The thing is to grab the attention of the reader at the outset. And to do so, it is necessary to research

---

[20] Ideally, every job application entails a résumé, a cover letter, and in some cases additional materials, unless otherwise stated.

the organization and learn more about their mission because it all comes to how you can help them solve this specific problem in the advertisement.

Another sticky point in the cover letter is whom should be the recipient. Indeed, most if not all of the advertised positions do not say to whom the application should go. At the same time, human resources analysts claim that a cover letter that does not address properly the recipient is outright disqualified under the invalid pretext that the applicant is not addressing a specific person, and one might catch the wrong person for the application. All that creates confusion and puts the job seeker in an uncomfortable situation. Why would an administrative assistant or whoever receives the cover letter simply bounce a cover letter to his superior, the hiring manager? For some reason, this will not happen.

In hindsight, it is understandable that a person's name is highly connected to one's identity and individuality. As such, it is the one attribute that can grab attention. In addition, it is argued that it is a sign of recognition and respect all together. Dale Carnegie, in his seminal book about human relations, wrote, "A person's name is to him or her the sweetest and most important sound in any language." This issue should not be taken lightly.

If the name of the person the application needs to be sent to does not appear in the advertisement, the immediate move that you can take is use the company's LinkedIn profile. Once there, you may get some interesting leads to find the staff for whom you are looking. You may feel that you are playing against the rule by calling because there are some advertisements that mention clearly that they do not want any phone call, but your hands are tied there. In making these phone calls, the general rule is to be precise, brief, and polite. After all, such a proactive attitude can go a long way in demonstrating that you are interested in the position, and this can make a difference. After finding out to whom the application needs to be sent, use either "Mr." or "Ms." with their family name as a salutation.

However, if for some reason the organization refuses to disclose the information you are seeking, you may use an alternatives like "To Whom It May Concern." Depending on the opening, it is suggested to aim higher than the hiring manager.[21]

---

[21] Templates are available at the end of the book, though they are meant only for examples.

I could not close out this section without briefly mentioning the ongoing debate about whether the résumé or the cover letter is the most important in the application package. I would not like to rehash the pros and cons of each argument, but in my view, I believe that each of them is important in its own right. That is why it is advisable to stand by what the employer requires and give the same amount of endeavor in the writing both documents.

Last but not least, you must read, reread, and spell-check the final draft of the cover letter before sending it. If necessary, get it read by friends. It may seem a lot of fuss, but it is worth its weight in gold. There is a reason why the saying goes that the devil is in the details, meaning that the difference between two applications hinges on details.

In order to increase the odds for an interview, in addition to using active verbs to describe your achievements, you need to end your cover letter on a high and exciting note that will spur the reviewer to take action in your favor.[22]

Before you send the cover letter and the résumé, more and more analysts recommend that initial contact be made by the recruiter. In a polite tone of voice, begin by saying, "I don't want to trouble you, but I would like to speak to …" This works in any circumstance. Then explain briefly why you are calling. You may be directed to the hiring manager. Then tell the manager how excited you are about the position, mentioning your solid background and how you can positively add to the staff. In case the person at the end of the line is not necessary the hiring manager but can give the name of one to whom the cover can be addressed, it is also fine because at least you have a name as an insider contact to express your enthusiasm for the company. Why should you go through all this trouble instead of simply following the herd by sending a cover letter and a résumé as a reply to the job posting? The answer is simple: employers tend to value qualities like boldness, confidence, and grit in candidates.

The diagram below provides an overview of the different sections in a cover letter, including contact information, why you are applying and are qualified, spacing, font choice, signature, and more.

---

[22] https://zety.com/blog/how-to-end-a-cover-letter.

Networking

We often hear that our economy is knowledge based, but at the same time we can say with confidence that it is in our networks-based economy. The saying goes, "It is not what you know but whom you know." The saying is even truer when it comes to finding a job.

The Merriam-Webster Online Dictionary defines *networking* as "the exchange of information or services among individuals, groups, or institutions." Yet it says further that it means specifically "the cultivation of productive relationships for employment or business."[23] Another online dictionary, the Cambridge Dictionary, is straightforward and precise. According to this resource, *networking* implies "the process of meeting and talking to a lot of people, especially in order to get information that can help someone."

Yet in the context of this guide, both definitions do not fit exactly, because they do not highlight the fact that networking consists of establishing solid, professional connections to specific individuals in specific places for future mutual professional benefits. It is building and nurturing long-lasting relationships. As such, it differs from the simple fact of mingling with other people at social encounters. What is job networking, then?

Job networking basically refers to meeting people with the intent to build and maintain professional relations that can hopefully result in a job opportunity. Several experts in the field agree that over 70 percent of job seekers land their jobs through connections, whereas others put this number anywhere between 80 and 85 percent.[24] According to the guru of career advice, Hal Lancaster, "Networking remains the No. 1 cause of job attainment." We are all aware that having someone put in a word for us or formally recommend us for a position has never disappeared from recruitment practices. But why has securing a position through networking been blown so much out of proportion?

Some argue that the so-called hidden job market—the fact that jobs go without being advertised—is responsible for that. Then again, one might ask what motivates the hidden job market. In reality, the basic reason identified by analysts is that whenever employers have the choice, they

---

[23] https://www.merriam-webster.com/dictionary/networking.

[24] https://www.payscale.com/career-news/2017/04/many-jobs-found-networking.

prefer co-opting their hires to save publicity, money, and time. They are also often pressed for time. Yet one reason that goes unnoticed is the fact that most employers feel comfortable working with people they get from both inside and outside referrals as an implicit security.

Beat the Odds When Networking

"If you want to gather honey, don't kick over the beehive" is the principle one of the timeless best sellers by Dale Carnegie, *How to Win Friends and Influence People*. It addresses the countereffects of criticizing. When we find fault with others or disapprove of their deeds in a disparaging way, we cannot expect them to be on our side. Carnegie is true in saying that even when the criticism is justified, as human beings, our "pride and vanity" prevent us from admitting that we are wrong because whenever our pride is hurt, we have a tendency to find ways to justify ourselves.

As true as this principle is for breeding sympathy, it also applies to networking. For most of us, the sticking point is how to network.

Assuming that patience is basically the virtue of sticking to a goal in spite of the difficulties and regardless of the amount of time it takes to achieve it, networking should be viewed as the epitome of that quality. As a matter of fact, the first quality of a good networker is patience. For one, all great things take time before they evolve and reach their full potential, and that is true of networking. In this, it differs from simply mingling at social events. On the contrary, networking is a longtime commitment with the aim to maintaining long-term and meaningful connections.

The time factor is all the more important given that we do not have the power to control the schedules of the people with whom we want to connect. Therefore, showing patience and understanding with them is a sign that we value and respect their privacy, which necessarily works in our favor.

The second rule to keep in mind is that networking is a two-way street, meaning that you have to bring something to the professional or social table if you want to make a positive and long-lasting impression on your counterpart. In your case, it hinges on a number of factors: your knowledge of the field, the relevance of your questions, how useful you might be in the short or long run, and your keen interest to keep contact with the prospective network. If you don't reciprocate, all these contacts will be going down the drain.

On the other hand, a better way of connecting to these busy people (if they seem to be so) would be to play the advice card. Who would not like to offer expertise in one's field? Remember we all like to talk about our achievements, particularly how we have reached the social ladder. To this end, it is necessary to search beforehand the people you will be dealing with at these gatherings, but if you really do not have any idea who they may be, you will be better off listening with keen interest to your interlocutors and asking them exciting questions about their achievements that will keep them talking. Who knows? Maybe with a healthy dose of confidence and optimism, you will end up striking a long-term relationship, which may blossom into mentorship and coaching.

The other challenge that may arise is how to keep and develop these useful connections. From my own experiences, human beings react more positively when the emotional side is targeted. This means that simple tokens like remembering their birthdays and sending Christmas and New Year's messages are deeply appreciated. These actions make them feel that not only have you not forgot them but also they still matter to you as human beings, not simply as opportunity mills. And most important, try to give before asking for anything.

Your other best bet for networking for professional purposes is to tap into alumni resources. Alumni are men and woman who attended or graduated from a particular school, college, or university. At a point in time, universities have understood the power of the alumni, and thus through their career services, they are trying to leverage alumni's connections not only to create and enhance various initiatives (including mentoring, coaching, shadow experiences, internships, placement, and full-time jobs for students) but also to increase and diversify their fundraising activities. Alumni can also offer valuable advice to students requesting informational interviews.

Finally, alumni can prove to be of an invaluable help when it comes to connecting and coaching students on social media like LinkedIn. But then again, reaching out to alumni for any sort of favors must be part of a give-and-take process. An analyst wrote, "It is easier to establish rapport if you seek to add value to people's lives. The more value you add, the more likely they will return the favor."

Where to Network?

There are numerous opportunities to network professionally. The first part of this guide mentioned a few, which include internships, volunteering, community activities, churches, mosques, clubs, and social events. Connecting to experts in one field for professional purposes is not the primary goal of the first ones, but there are specific venues that are meant to serve this purpose. Career fairs, trade shows, and conferences fall into this category. As young professionals transitioning into the workforce, the tendency is to rely heavily on family network. But the thing is these events are the real opportunities, even for college students, to set up their own lists of professionals who can prove critical in their careers.

In this regard, occurrences like trade shows, career fairs, workshops, conferences, and professional conventions might put a little more strain on your budget, but they are worth the try. One thing to keep in mind is that each happening must be viewed in its uniqueness in the sense that it provides a live opportunity for you to talk to all these experts. In this respect, the question that I ask myself every time before signing up for them is "Where else would I meet these guys if not here?" This is another incentive to go to these professional events.

On the other hand, you cannot expect to have the slightest success in a social setting if you do not equip yourself with the right marketing tools. Business cards and an elevator pitch are unbeatable in this respect.

First, you need to have your professional business cards printed with your name, title, and contact information. Carry them everywhere you may interact with professionals. Remember that even though people are highly visible through the flooding of social media, nothing will replace the positive effect of first impression through the exchange of business cards, to say nothing of the credibility and confidence that it imparts to the card owner.

In addition to that, it is highly regarded as a sign of professionalism and preparedness to give one's business cards during any encounter at an event. In Japan, for instance, it is considered rude to not share your business card with your counterpart as the first gesture when meeting them, even before shaking hands. The formality is unparalleled when the business card has to be received with both hands and examined before putting it in one's pocket.

One last thing to mind before going to network events is to be well prepared. Résumés and cover letters are necessary, but career fairs and background information about those whom you will be dealing with and business cards are always needed. The combination of both provides an exciting opportunity to interact productively with the professionals.

Nurturing and Grooming Relationships

We all come into contact with many people, either in our jobs or in a casual way, and this is more common for those who build connections for professional purposes. Nonetheless, not all of them end up as friends. Actually, most people have a hard time turning contacts into valuable, productive connections. What generally happens is that in the networking process, we do not take the time to focus on a lasting relationship that yields dividends in the future. The bad tendency is to expect to yield the benefits of networking right away. It is a common trait to ask for an internship or full job to someone we met only couple of weeks earlier at an event. Of course, unless we have been recommended, what naturally ensues is a rebuke because networking is a long-term process. Asking for a favor from people we hardly know scares them away. The lesson to learn here is that nothing happens overnight. Life does not work that way. The fact is nothing can be done in a snap. Like a baby who grows steadily from day one till it can stand on its own feet, all kinds of relationships need time to develop before reaching their full potential. With that said, they need to be nurtured and groomed till they mature.

A recommended way to engage in an ongoing relationship after a networking event is to follow up with a memorable thank-you note.[25] As impressive as a thank-you note might be, if it comes as a single-shot act, it will certainly not suffice to lastingly connect two people. I believe that the most important values that need to be nurtured here are confidence and trust. To achieve that, there is no need to go to great lengths; small gestures like sharing a cup of coffee or having lunch together are enough to start getting to know each other. It comes down to exerting patience, perseverance, and gentleness toward your goal.

---

[25] How memorable and heartfelt should that message be to compel the connection to remember us? That is the question.

You may build a LinkedIn profile as a way to increase your visibility and skill set, and you can engage with more professionals inside and outside your area of expertise. The fact of the matter is that with every task you undertake, you must do it to the best of your ability.

The Interview

Imagine that after following the steps described in this guide, your résumé and cover letter grab the attention of the hiring managers, and they decide to take you to the next level of the process with an interview. However, be aware that the interview is only half the battle, and for some reason it is the hardest part of the process. Failing it after all the work you put into the preparation is likely to affect you badly. For this reason, before even thinking about how to prepare for this important and difficult stage of the hiring process, you need to know what the job interview is and what it is not.

The Online Collins Dictionary defines the job interview as "a formal meeting at which someone is asked questions in order to find out if they are suitable for a post of employment."[26] Actually, it is called a face-to-face interview because the interview entailing the screening process had already begun with the reception of the application materials sent by the applicant. It is a reality that an employer will not offer you a job interview because of your beautiful eyes, but because after reviewing the batch of applications, the person noticed that your qualifications, skills, and experience match the job requirements, and so the company decided to reach out for an interview. As a matter of fact, most of the job listings have always been clear about the fact that only the candidates of interest, the short-listed ones, will be contacted further.[27]

Preliminary contacts interview may be taken place on the phone before setting a face-to-face interaction on Skype or other visual enabled platforms. The number of these initial contacts and the people involved depends on the size of the company or organization, but in some cases, an on-site interview is the last step of the process.

---

[26] https://www.collinsdictionary.com/dictionary/english/job-interview.

[27] There also numerous cases where companies contact the candidates to let them know that they prefer other candidates in the hiring process.

The objective of this exercise is twofold, assessing both your hard and soft skills. First, the employer wants to make sure that you possess the skills described in the job requirements. Through a series of questions addressing those skills, the company's aim is to confirm or reverse the information laid in your cover letter and résumé.

Second, the company wants to learn more about what kind of person you are. Then the so-called soft skills come into play. You may be intellectually skilled, but will you be able to adapt to the work environment? In other words, will you be a good fit? Recruiters don't want to make a bad decision about a new hire.

Types of Interviews

With this said, there are three different forms of interviews.[28] Depending on the position and the size of the organization, you may be facing a one-to-one interview, a panel interview, or a competency interview. The one-to-one interview, the most common, is where only the interviewer and the interviewee face each other. The interviewer conducts the interview process in a conversational tone by asking both technical and general questions. General questions address the soft skills, which include problem solving, interpersonal skills, and communications abilities. The technical questions try to see if you satisfy the requirements of the job listing in terms of experience and qualifications.

The second format is the panel interview. It is a session in which an applicant faces a group of people, generally from the organization, conducting the recruitment. It can also happen that people outside the organization are requested. The aim of this form of job interview is not only to gain more insight into the abilities of the candidate but also to reduce the risk of making a bad hire because at the end of the session, the decision of whether to hire the candidate or not lies upon this committee.

Compared to the one-on-one format, the panel interview may require other follow-up interviews with higher ranks or the direct supervisor.

---

[28] Interviews exist in different formats. Apart from the above-highlighted ones that are commonly used by hiring managers, there are specialized types like case interviews, stress interviews, and technical interviews.

The good news is that the other interviews following the one held by the committee come as a formality; your performance with the panel is the most determinant.

The last interview style is the competency interview. Also referred to as situational, behavioral, or competency questions, the competency-based interview typically assesses a candidate's key competencies. The behavioral interview mainly tests the situational experiences of the applicant. In other words, if a candidate does not have such experience, it would be impossible for him to find an answer. For that reason, it provides valuable insights into a candidate's soft skill set. The rationale behind this type of interview is that if a job applicant has already found himself in the situation described by the question, he will feel comfortable answering the question. It is hailed as the most advanced and difficult forms of interviews, but if it probes the applicant's past experiences related to specific professional situations, it also acts as a predictor of how he may react and handle similar situations in the future. Most important, the employer is probing his ability to deal with pressure and work style in unanticipated situations.

Although this style is said to be mostly used in cases where previous working experience is not essential or lacking, manager positions require often this style of interview more often because of the responsibilities involved in them, so technically any graduate making his debut in the workforce should expect such questions.

Acing the Interview with a Good Preparation

Knowing the different types of interview is a fact, but preparing efficiently for them is a horse of a different color. Job interviews are a big deal. That is why we can never overemphasize the role that preparation plays in the process. In other circumstances, interview as part of oral presentations would have passed as a formality, but not in the job-hunting process.

First off, you have to read and fully understand the job description and requirements, specifically the desirable skills. It is not enough to be invited for an interview because reaching this stage of the process has set your application as a fit for further consideration. Still, it does not mean that you understood what the employer is looking for or addressed the core competencies in your cover letter. On the other hand, you have no idea how you place yourself against the other candidates in the running. This is one more reason to take this step very seriously and comprehend the competencies explicitly and implicitly displayed in the job description. As previously mentioned, the interview will generally be a combination of a bit of general, technical, skill, and behavioral questions, with an emphasis on competency-based questions in positions with a large scope. The behavioral-based interviews are the trickiest and seem to be hard nuts to crack because of their structured nature targeting a specific skill or competency in the job listing, so we will focus our effort on this specific type.

Second, it is necessary to make a list of the variety of skills and competencies listed in the job description and then address them with specific examples. The good news is that those examples do not necessarily need to stem from past work experience; real life experiences or extracurricular engagement activities are equally welcome.

In any event, regardless the type of interview you may be facing, the best way to prevent any nasty surprise is to apply the STAR approach, which gives the interviewer an overview of the array of your skills.[29]

STAR is an acronym that stands for Situation, Task, Action, and Result. Others may term it as CAR, for Challenge, Actions, and Results. No matter what it is called, in the field of communication, it is an efficient

---

[29] Originally developed by Hagymas Laszlo, professor of language at the University of München, and Dr. Alexander Botos, chief curator of the National Institute of Economic and Social Research, SOARA (Situation, Objective, Action, Results, Aftermath) is a job interview technique used by interviewers to gather all the relevant information about a specific capability that the job requires. It is similar to the STAR technique, although it's slightly more involved.

Situation: The interviewer wants you to present a recent challenge and situation in which you found yourself.

Objective: What did you have to achieve? The interviewer will be looking to see what you were trying to achieve from the situation.

Action: What did you do? The interviewer will be looking for information on what you did, why you did it, and what the alternatives were.

Results: What was the outcome of your actions? What did you achieve through your actions? Did you meet your objectives?

Aftermath: What did you learn from this experience? Have you used this learning since?

method to convey clearly and concisely one's message. Experts recommend it for answering behavioral interview questions because it appears to be the designated approach to structure one's response when it comes to discussing the specific situation, specific task performed, the action taken, and the result achieved. This is the stage on which you have to display your skills you have been accumulating over the year. In a nutshell, the only thing you have to do is to impress the recruiter by strutting your best stuff.

The Situation part sets the stage by providing a backdrop context, followed by the various Tasks required and Activities actually performed within the framework of the duties and responsibilities; it's closed by the Results achieved.

The following are typical competency-based questions and how to deal with them using the STAR methodology.

"Tell me about a time you had a conflict on a team project."

"S/T (Situation/Task)

- Briefly describe the context for the conflict that arose. Provide just enough background information for context. Point out the responsibilities and actions taken, and the end results.

Being on One's Best during the Interview

Job interviews seem frightening, no matter how well prepared the interview is. If most job hunters can dodge it, I bet that they will not hesitate to do so. Unfortunately, it is the common fate of all who are searching for a job. However, it can be different with a very good preparation. After the first seconds of stage fright, the candidate should be able to regain his composure. Yet, all the above mentioned would not serve any purpose if the candidate does not have the right mind-set during the interview.

First and foremost, the interviewee needs to establish rapport the second he walks through the door of the interviewer. According to studies, hiring managers make the favorable or unfavorable decision to hire a candidate within the first five minutes of the interview. I am not saying that if you do not have a knack for connecting with others or a sense of trust and understanding within minutes, you have to fake it. What I mean is that with a smiling and confident face, you create an inviting and positive atmosphere, and you set the unique tone for connection with the interviewer. Because it is in the best interest of the interviewee to lighten the mood of the conversation, some experts recommend kicking off with memorable information they collected about the company instead of waiting for the interviewer to beginning with common chitchat. Beyond the immediate fact that the interviewee is showing that he is not solely caring about how well he will be doing on the interview, he is showing his human side. After all, you will be working with human peers with whom you have to get along. Statistics say that professionals spend at least 33 percent of the time working, with the rest being devoted to family life and vacations, so you had better dispel the doubt that you might not be a fit for the rest of the team.

Another easy way to build rapport is to remember the name of the interviewer. It might be a bit hard in a panel interview to come by the names of all the speakers, particularly in an interview setting where introduction is made quickly and the interviewee might be stressed, but it is a good idea to make an effort to recall those names when answering questions.

The next thing to do once the candidate steps inside the interview room is to shake hands firmly and confidently with the interviewer if the interviewer extends a hand. When shaking hands with the interviewer, one must maintain eye contact. Why are these gestures so relevant? By demonstrating such an attitude, the interviewee is proving oneself right and fit for the position. Believe me, employers prefer to deal with self-confident collaborators.

Finally, when providing answers to the interviewer's questions, no matter how difficult or intricate they are, the interviewee needs to remain calm; speak slowly and with an audible, firm, and cohesive voice; and keep one's hands in his lap. Nobody expects an interviewee to be 100 percent ready for an interview or to have all the answers, but self-assurance that originates in the seriousness of the preparation is everything. Each job interview has its own goals and characteristics, but overall the competency-based questions tend to follow a generic trend aiming at assessing the candidate's skills in situ. Here are a few of them:

> How do you ensure that you maintain good working relationships with your coworkers?

Give us an example of a situation where you had to deal with a conflict. What was the situation? What was your role? What was the outcome? How do you influence people in situations where there are conflicting agendas?

Tell us about a situation where you made a decision and then changed your mind. What was the situation? What did you do? What was the outcome?

Can you give us an example of a situation in which you took charge of a situation? What was the situation? What was your strategy? What was the outcome?

In many cases, the interviewers will start with a general question and then follow up with more specific, example-based questions. Here are some examples.

How do you communicate instructions to others?

How do you manage tasks?

Give us an example of a situation where you had a fundamental disagreement with one of your coworkers. How did you handle it?

What would your coworkers say about you?

It may happen that the interviewer has never experienced the situation alluded in the question by the interviewer. The interviewee can still draw from one's experiences similar evidence by focusing on the competence that the interviewer is aiming at.

Interviews are structured in such a way that when they are drawing to an end, the interviewer asks the interviewee whether the interviewee has questions. I mentioned above that one way to control the process is to start asking questions to the recruiter as a manner of bewildering him or catching him off guard. But for some reason, if the interviewee did not have the chance to place his questions at the beginning of the interview, he still holds all the cards in his hands. What he has to do is to use the opportunity wisely. For instance, the interviewee can ask the recruiter how he did on the answers.

The odds that the interviewer says the interviewee did well are high, but it may be as way to get rid of the person. Instead, the interviewee is well aware that there might be some questions that he failed or at least is not satisfied with the answer. Then he can be honest and recognize that he did not do well on this on that question, and he can take this opportunity to give the right answer. Otherwise, the interviewee may ask questions involving the challenges of the position. For example, he can ask, "What are the main challenges of this position? What am I expected to deliver as result in the first two or three months?" The surefire question that will reveal the core qualities associated with the position would be, "If you could design the ideal candidate for this position from the ground up, what would he or she be like?" Like above, where the candidate is trying to catch up on his answers, this question is definitely one that will reveal the recruiter as an open book. The ultimate goal is to demonstrate to the potential employer that you are excited and motivated to pick up the gauntlet, and this leaves a very positive impression.

Handling Tricky Questions

As previously defined, the interview is the encounter between a potential recruiter and a job hunter, with the former assessing the abilities of the latter to see if he is a match, and the latter finding out whether the organization is the right fit. For some unknown reasons, there are some open-ended questions that are guaranteed to surface in most job interviews, no matter what the industry, experience level, and job type. The funniest part of the deal is that most candidates miss the point about these questions because they do not know what the interviewer is really driving at.

The first and most common is "Tell me about yourself" By this question, the interviewer is not inviting the candidate to blurt out his life story or rehash a résumé. In reality, this question generally succeeds the traditional "How are you?" while the interviewer is offering a seat to the interviewer. He wants to know how the candidate's background experience, knowledge, and skills are pertinent to the opening. This question is an opportunity for the interviewee to convince the recruiter that he has found the perfect hire for the position. In a concise and enthusiastic manner, try to summarize your unique selling points that are relevant to the job through past experiences.[30]

Unfortunately, interview settings are where first impression matters most, and each candidate's aim would be to make an extremely strong first impression. As an opening question, the answer may reflect either positively or negatively on the rest of the interview process. Experts would recommend "the Present-Past-Future formula." Like in the STAR pattern, this style of describing one's strengths begins with the current role of the candidate, and then it continues by making a slight foray into his past experiences and how they prove relevant to the position. It finishes with his unique contribution to the position at hand. Below are three ways of dealing with this question to help you get a sense of what is expected.

"Well, I'm currently an account executive at Smith, where I handle our top performing client. Before that, I worked at an agency where I was on three different major national healthcare brands. Although I really enjoyed the work that I did, I'd love the chance to dig in much deeper with one specific healthcare company, which is why I'm so excited about this opportunity with Metro Health Center."[31]

"I began my career in retail management, but a few years ago, I was drawn to the healthcare space. I've always been skilled at bringing people together and working toward common goals. My experience successfully leading teams and managing stores led me to consider administration, and I've been building a career as a driven health administrator for the last four years."

"In my current role at XYZ Medical Center, the efficiency of the office has been a personal focus—especially as it

---

[30] On a side note, it is worth mentioning that when stepping through the interviewer's office door, the interviewee has to wait till one is offered to sit down.

[31] https://www.coursehero.com/file/14220680/How-to-Answer.

relates to patient outcomes. I set and oversee goals related to department budget and patient volume. Last year, I worked with our IT department to implement a communication system for scheduling procedures and protocols to ensure that all departments were adequately staffed at all times. With our new online scheduling portal, we increased communication efficiency by 20 percent. To stay informed about their ongoing concerns, I hold regular meetings with physicians, nurses, and other healthcare staff. In my role, I also manage marketing and advertising efforts on behalf of the center. I've been really enjoying that part of my work, and I'm especially interested in bringing the experience I've gained as well as my commitment to efficiency to the team at ABC Health. Outside of the office, I'm an avid reader, and I love to hike. On weekends, you might find me at the local bookstore or exploring hiking trails in the area."[32]

Another thoughtful way to answer this question is "Well, obviously I could tell you about lots of things, and if I'm missing what you want, please let me know. But the three things I think are most important for you to know about me are [your selling points]. I can expand on those a little, if you'd like."

Interviewers will always say, "Sure, go ahead."

Then you say, "Well, regarding the first point, [give your example]. And when I was working for [company], I [example of another selling point]."

Some variations of this question are "Walk me through your background," "Tell me something about yourself that's not on your résumé," and "How would you describe yourself?"

Other series of questions of the same sort encompass the following: "What qualities make you a great fit for this position?"

Let us say that you came to the interview all geared up. Before answering this question, take a deep breath and think of what constitutes your unique selling points that match the job requirements, which means

---

[32] https://www.indeed.com/career-advice/interviewing/interview-question-tell-me-about-yourself.

that you did your homework by thoroughly reviewing the duties, purpose, and responsibilities involved in the role for which you are applied.

"Why are you interested in the role?" Centuries ago, Confucius said, "Choose a job you love, and you will never have to work a day in your life." When applied to today's fast-moving economy that requires high adaptability and flexibility, this saying seems obsolete. However, its philosophy still resonates with all candidates who apply to a position. It is because the applicant identifies himself with at least one of the core requirements that his cover letter and résumé caught the attention of the hiring manager. Drawing on that, he can put forward why the position is particularly exciting for him and how he intends to contribute. Another manner to answer cleverly to this question is to indicate that you have arrived at a point in your career where you are looking for a new challenge, that the role at hand is the best one.

"Why are you interested in the company or the industry?" This question may confuse the interviewee because it's obvious. But the employer's perspective is to tie the candidate's selling points and future goals to the company's corporate mission and vision, which boils down to the fact the interviewee spent time researching the company. In an attempt to outclass the competition, the candidate may find out anecdotes about the company, all of which can build rapport with the recruiter and prove the interest of the candidate.

"Out of all the other candidates, why should we hire you?" or **"What makes you the best fit for this position?"** Either of these questions is tricky. It is impossible for a candidate to compare with other fellow candidates, so he can only hope that he came best prepared. On the other hand, this feeling has to be grounded in facts. In the best of cases, he needs to highlight how the hard and soft skills, including transferable skills, combine to make the candidate a unique specimen for the opening. Here is a sample answer: "Based on what you've said and from the research I've done, your company is looking for an administrative assistant who is strong in interpersonal skills and in tech skills. I believe my experience aligns well with that and makes me a great fit. I'm an effective communicator who is skilled in giving oral presentations, speaking on the phone, and communicating via email. I'm also fluent in a number of relevant software programs, including content management systems and spreadsheet suites. I'd really love to bring my diverse skill set to your company."[33]

"What are your greatest strengths?" We all have weaknesses. By asking this question, the recruiter is not blaming you for having them. He wants to know how you are working to correct them. It is easier to point our weaknesses because we would like to be humble, but it is hard to exhibit our strengths at the risk of sounding pretentious. Still, in the job interview, you cannot afford to hide your light under the bushel. Here are some other examples to tailor to your values that make you unique for the job.

Managing the "Do You Have Questions?" Part of the Interview

As a rule of thumb, when the interview is moving toward the end, the interviewer may ask the interviewee whether he has questions. It is not always that way, though. As an analyst suggested, every proactive job hunter should apply right away and start the discussion even before the hiring manager asks his first question. It can throw the interviewer out of balance, push him out of his comfort zone, and give an edge to the interviewee. But if the interviewee is asked to save them for the end, that's fair enough.

However, when it is right for the applicant to learn more about the position, specifically if the job description is vague, it is also true that the tactic of the interviewee attacking with questions means that those questions need to be relevant to the context.

Nonetheless, it is high time to dispel all the misconceptions about the interview. Interview settings are not classrooms where an instructor is sitting at an end of a table and a student is at the other one. Rather, interviews are an exchange and a conversation, not quizzes or exams, because employer and candidate have vested interests in the process. On the one hand, there is an employer who is eager to find the right fit for the position, and on the other hand is a candidate who is trying to get hold of a position for which he has been working.

---

[33] https://www.thebalancecareers.com/why-should-we-hire-you-best-answers-2061261.

All in all, the hiring manager may not have the upper hand in the process, and it is an opportunity for the candidate to assess whether the organization is the right one.

Well-prepared candidates should never see interviews as question-answer sessions but as two-way streets. When the interviewer asks the interviewee whether there are questions, he is not acting according to procedure—he is testing how informed the candidate is and if she did her homework before coming to the interview. Then, it is the interviewee's very moment to rise and shine with thoughtful questions as a way to display self-confidence, motivation, interest, and knowledge about the company and the position at hand.

Still, it is best to avoid asking generic questions about company structure, challenges of the role, and potential career path—questions easily spotted either on the website of the company or in the job description. Rather, be specific and constructive to show that you are a forward and proactive thinker. The pointer here is to be set above the fray. Recruiting expert James Caan recommends asking challenging questions: "What are your experiences within the company? As an interviewer, what qualities do you look for that you personally feel fit into the organization? What weaknesses have other employees with similar backgrounds to me had in the company? How have their experiences played out to their advantage? What I do better than my predecessor?"

On the other end of the spectrum, because the interviewee wants to make the best impression possible, he should ask all questions that cross his mind. It would not be a good idea to view the "Do you have questions?" part of the interview that way. On the contrary, it should be used wisely to catch up on some of the questions that the candidate may have failed. Here is the experience of a job candidate I am paraphrasing: "We were almost at the end of the interview, and I knew that I screwed it all along. Then they asked me whether I had questions for them. I was about to speak when an idea popped up into my mind. Why not take advantage of that moment to patch up things? Then I went on and on, highlighting the whole range of mistakes I'd made during the interview and providing the right answers. In the end, I received an offer."

I have to repeat that if the candidate had not put a significant amount of time and hard work into being prepared for this interview, it would not have been possible to redeem himself.

Salary Negotiation

Not all job interviews end up with a salary proposition. But if it happens, it a sign that the interviewee made a hit and is getting onboard. The recruiter may be so much impressed by the interviewee's output that he might want to discuss salary right away.

Nevertheless, what comes as natural for an experienced and well-informed professional may be baffling for a college student who is entering the workforce for the first time. Time and time again come the age-old questions: What are your salary expectations? What do you expect to make?

Nowadays, most job applicants do not set foot in an interview room without doing research about the salary ranges they are worth.

Nevertheless, because each candidate has no idea how other interviewees will propose, or the total budget for the position, it is best for the clever candidate to hold his ground first. The most important thing here to remember is not to make the first move and put a figure on the table because if so, either he undersells himself (meaning that he loses money), or oversells himself (and is denied the job because the hiring manager might find the range too high). If a similar candidate with the same credentials proposes less, that person might be chosen over the first one.

Under these circumstances, unless the interviewee is forced to put forward a figure, one way to proceed is to appeal the moral sense of the hiring manager. Here is an example of answer to such a question. "You are aware of the responsibilities involved in this role, and I am confident that Company Z is a respectable company that treats its employees fairly so that they can perform well their duties. So in line with all that, whatever you have planned for the position, I will go with it."

In any event, before leaving the interview room, it is best to end on a positive note by expressing to the manager how excited you still are for the position, including something you learned about the position. Be enthusiastic about it, saying thanks and how grateful you are for their time.

Shake hands if possible and then ask about the next steps. All that shows your keen interest for the role.

Tying Loose Ends When Going to the Interview

What to Wear for the Interview?

In an article titled "Why is it weird if men dress like women, but if women dress like men, it's normal?" Leslie Ellen Szczesniak argues that although unisex fashion is commonly admitted for women, cross-dressing for men is rarely accepted even if it reflects the hidden desire to look like the other sex.[34]

Following this trend, it is recommended for job candidates to dress conventionally, even conservatively if need be. In other words, they should dress in a way that is not distracting. It is fact that different companies may advocate for different dress codes, but it seems unacceptable to see males coming to an interview with a ponytail, earrings, or even tattoos. I do not mean that tattoos should be prohibited. But for those who have them in a glaring way, I believe that they should hide it for that day. It may disservice them to give a bad first impression to the recruiter. The ideal situation would be to find out about the particular dress code of the company or organization with which you are interviewing. But in most cases, it is recommended to wear a business suit for men. The same goes for women, except that they may wear either a pair of trousers or a skirt.

Furthermore, the interviewee needs to be well groomed on that day and arrive before the interview time. It is better to be at the interview place well in advance than arrive late. Being late makes a very bad impression of sloppiness and inability to manage time.

Customized Thank-You Note after the Interview

Getting through the interview is not an end in itself because it is time to write a thank-you note. It is recommended to send a personalized

[34] https://www.quora.com/Why-is-it-weird-if-men-dress-like-women-but-if-women-dress-like-men-its-normal.

thank-you note to each interviewer individually, ideally within twenty-four hours following the interview, regardless of the type of interview. It is a way to stand out from the crowd. The general principle remains the same. All human beings like feeling special, unique, and appreciated. They are sensitive to recognition and consideration. With this basic truth in mind, the thank-you note appears as a postinterview catch-up opportunity to reconnect with the hiring manager. It is not that the follow-up note alone has the power to change the outcome of a bad interview, but among equally good candidates, a thank-you note is a recommended way to make the employer remember you favorably, especially if you refer to something you mentioned that moved the interviewer. In addition to that, it is a means to express your gratitude to the hiring manager for giving you the unique opportunity to show them your strengths and interest in the position. At some point, add details that make you stand above the fray and that you might have omitted during the interview. The wording should include phrases like "I appreciate," "I am grateful for," and "I am thankful for." The most important thing here is to put into a personal touch that leaves a memorable trail.

With this said, thank-you notes must be kept short and to the point, ending with "I look forward to hearing back from you."

Takeaways

The first job search tools that the applicant needs to develop are the résumé and the cover letter. Both tools are not one-off documents and one size fits all. Instead, they have to be crafted and tailored to the job opening. In both cases, it is important and highly recommended to thoroughly read and understand all the requirements listed in the job description, specifically the so-called core requirements. Ideally, all the qualifications and specifications in the job listing should be addressed, specifically if the applicant wants to beat the ATS.

The cover letter should begin with an attention-grabbing formula and end on a high note, inviting the hiring manager to take action. In this regard, there are two main questions that the applicant needs to answer in a relevant manner:

How can I be original and catch the reader's attention enough to encourage him or her to read through my cover letter?

In what way can I show my skills my skills and experience so as to match the skills and experience needed to do the job?

Finally, the cover letter has to be well formatted, proofread, and addressed to a specific person.

PART III

The Bullhead Brewer

The Art of Making Opportunities Happen

Statistics say that over 70 percent of jobs are not listed, and some studies say it's even 80 percent. For more accurate figures, analysts say that out of 3.7 million job openings in 2012, 80 percent of them were never advertised.[35] In the case that these openings are officially advertised, for transparency purposes, they are actually filled either internally or through networking. As far as networking is concerned, it makes up to 60 percent of new hires. Making connections for professional purpose remains "the most effective path." The term professionals use to explain this trend is the hidden job market. In reality, the word *hidden* here has nothing to do with any kind of secrecy or lack of transparency. It is all related to the practice of recruiting their employees in a way that eludes public attention. The following is a letter a job seeker asked Liz Rayan:

Dear Liz,

You talk about the hidden job market. I have been hearing that term for a few years, but I do not really know what it means. What is the hidden job market, and how do I get into it? I have been filling out online job applications for

---

[35] https://www.forbes.com/sites/jacquelynsmith/2013/04/17/7-things-you-probably-didnt-know-about-your-job-search/#75fc9bed3811.

months now and barely getting a nibble, even though I have seven years of project management experience certification and a résumé full of great brand names.

Thanks for your advice, Liz.

Noah

Here is the reply from Liz:

Dear Noah,

There is a hidden job market. There are more jobs- or more accurately, assignments- that go unadvertised than jobs that are posted to the public. There is a lot of work that needs to be done.

Individuals, corporations, start-ups and not-for-profit agencies need help of various kinds. They have problems. Government agencies have problems. A lot of work is performed outside the standard full-time employment framework, and those projects are entrance ramps to the hidden job market.[36]

The reply by Liz to Noah echoes a thoughtful Bible verse: "Then he said to his disciples, 'The harvest is plentiful, but the laborers are few; therefore, pray earnestly to the Lord of the harvest to send out laborers into his harvest.'"[37]

Between Jesus exhorting his disciples to reach out to the lost souls and Liz teaching Noah about the infinite job opportunities that he simply needs to extend his hand to grasp them, the comparison highlights the sole idea that proactivity and hard work are the best policies. In fact, there is

---

[36] Liz Rayan is the founder and CEO of Human Workplace, a publishing and consulting firm. She is the author of *Reinvention Road Map: Break the Rules to Get the Job You Want and Career You Deserve.* https://www.forbes.com/sites/lizryan/2017/06/20/whats-the-hidden-job-market-and-how-do-i-get in/#53ad553157dc.

[37] The Bible, King James Version (Oxford UP, 1998).

an urgent need for individuals willing to toll up their sleeves, rather than loiters, to work tirelessly toward achieving what matters, either conquering lost souls or digging up unposted or uncreated jobs. Equally, like Jesus, who sends his disciples to announce the good news to the billions of unchurched people, Liz is urging any job hunter to adopt an entrepreneur spirit to uncover the hidden job market.

With all this said, it is an obvious fact that the job market is highly dynamic, volatile, unpredictable, and constantly changing, with new businesses being created and old ones disappearing, let alone the tremendous amount of work the existing ones have to put out in order to stay in business. The good news is that all this turmoil can work to the advantage of the smart job seeker. My point is that if there is a hidden job market in which employers tap to co-opt their new hires, there are also numerous unsatisfied or hidden needs in companies that need to be fulfilled. Companies and organizations, more than any commercial or social entities, are the most prone to have unlimited, and most often unmet, needs due to the very nature of their missions to serve others.

In the marketing jargon, hidden or latent needs are products or services that may solve customers' specific problems of which they are not aware. The same hidden needs that can be uncovered apply equally to companies and organizations owing to a competitive and constantly changing world. As such, the job seeker who can identify and address them has a real competitive advantage and will be sought after because he will be solving a problem (breakthrough products or services) that will help the company lead the field. All that the prospective job seeker needs is to have the entrepreneur mind in order to set himself as a job creator and not necessarily a job taker.

The Entrepreneur Mind-Set

In the late 1990s, I got the unique chance to read *Wealth and Poverty* by George Gilder. Hailed as a devotion to pure capitalism, the book sparked a debate, but after perusing the table of contents, I was struck by the contents of chapter five, "The Nature of Wealth." The author states that "work, indeed, is the root of wealth," and even what is generally termed a genius takes root in hard work and sweat. Once, a journalist asked Quincy Jones

Jr., the infamous American musician and record producer, what the secret of his great success was. He leaned back in his chair, smiled, and said that the so-called genius is made of 1 percent inspiration and 99 percent hard work.

In order to substantiate his argument, the author of *Wealth and Poverty* describes the life of a Lebanese family, the Zabians, who in almost a decade managed to make a fortune for themselves by dint of hard work and commitment, thus fulfilling their American dream.

> Ten years ago, a Lebanese family arrived in Lee, Massachusetts, with a few dollars and fewer words of English. The family invested the dollars in buying a woebegone and abandoned shop beside the road on the edge of town, and they started marketing vegetables. The man rose at five every morning to drive slowly a ramshackle truck a hundred miles to farms in the Connecticut Valley, where he purchased the best goods he could find as cheaply as possible to sell that morning in Lee.

In chapter twenty, "The Bullheaded Brewer," the author highlights the role that the entrepreneur spirit plays in the creation of economic wealth.

> In order to have growth, openness must be joined by a certain 'bull-headedness,' some Keynesian "animal spirits, and an essential optimism and willingness to risk. In order to take the hill, someone must dare first to charge the enemy bunker. Heroism, willingness to plunge into the unknown, in the hope that others will follow, is indispensable to all great human achievement.

This chapter is so relevant to our purpose that I am quoting a comment about it.

> The bullheaded brewer parable explanation for the entrepreneurial accelerator has been and continues to be an important factor in U.S. economic development. According to David McCord Wright, erstwhile Professor of Economics at the University of Georgia, there are three

reasons a brewer with sagging prices and/or sales volume might build a new brewery; (1) a better brew; (2) a cheaper brew; or (3) a prescient "bullheaded brewer" with chutzpah who may simply feel he or she is smarter than the market and whose courage and stimulus of construction can start the economy moving ala Say's Law.

Here, I am not talking about entrepreneurship in the literal sense of the word. I am viewing the entrepreneur as he who creates the job instead of seeking it. The point I want to make here is that the entrepreneurial spirit that the Zabian family adopted and displayed all along—meaning getting up very early and traveling all the way to collect the freshest fruits—is at the core of their success. The most interesting thing about the word is the undergirding idea. More and more people are advocating for a broader meaning of the word itself. They do not restrict it to the sphere of creating and running a business; it is part and parcel of the way "people do to take their career and dreams into their hands and lead it in the direction of their own choice. It's about building a life on your own terms." Addressed in this regard, the entrepreneurial spirit is part of any endeavor to change things or solving problems by creating value. In a competitive global market place striving for innovation to edge the competition, the entrepreneurial spirit is a much-sought-after quality, and graduate students who are searching for their first professional roles in the workforce can use the same attitude to land their dream jobs. Here is what Muhammad Yunus, the university professor who launched the Grameen Bank idea in the 1970s, said about the entrepreneurial mind-set: "Instead of going through life expecting to get a job, rather, we should be job *creators*." I am not sure whether he is speaking specifically to students, but it works. This sentence aligns so well with core skills like critical thinking, analysis and synthesis skills, and problem-solving skills that the university teaches the students.

The Qualities of an Entrepreneur

No matter what the study field or major is, being innovative and proactive is key to success in the job search process. In other words, what the students need here is the entrepreneurial spirit. Without being able to define exactly what the entrepreneurial spirit is, what we know for sure is that the entrepreneurial mind-set is broadly defined by a certain number of traits and attitudes. Most entrepreneurs tend to be changers rather than adapting the existing situation that does not satisfy them, all geared by the thinking of doing things better given the circumstances.

It is amazing how *entrepreneur* is no longer a term only reserved for those who are their own bosses.

A study revealed that "90 percent of professionals considered entrepreneurship as someone "who sees opportunities and pursues them" rather than "someone who starts a company."[38]

Actually, the entrepreneurial spirit is a mind-set. It's an attitude and approach to thinking and behaving that actively seeks out change, rather than waiting to adapt to change. It's a mind-set that embraces critical questioning, innovation, service, and continuous improvement. "We have to come up with ideas to generate leads, to create opportunities, and essentially own the overall pipeline of business."

According to Sara Sutton Fell, CEO and founder of FlexJobs,

> To me, an entrepreneurial spirit is a way of approaching situations where you feel empowered, motivated, and capable of taking things into your own hands. Companies that nurture an entrepreneurial spirit within their organization encourage their employees to not only see problems, solutions and opportunities, but to come up with ideas to do something about them.

For Michael Kerr, international business speaker, author, and president of Humor at Work, "It's about seeing the big picture and thinking like an owner … It's being agile, never resting on your laurels, shaking off the cloak of complacency and seeking out new opportunities. It's about taking ownership and pride in your organization."

That being so, all entrepreneurs share various features: passion, enthusiasm, vision, leadership, and problem-solving skills. These are essential to their success. I beg to insist on the last quality cited here,

---

[38] https://www.forbes.com/sites/danschawbel/2013/05/14/the-re-definition-of-entrepreneurship-and-rise-of-freedom-seeking-freelancers.

problem-solving skills. If problem solving is referred to as the "ability to solve problems in an effective and timely manner without any impediments. It involves being able to identify and define the problem, generating alternative solutions, evaluating and selecting the best alternative, and implementing the selected solution," then it is obvious that any entrepreneur must be equipped with this specific skill set because his core function is to see possibilities and solutions where the average person only sees annoyances and problems. The students are trained to be this way.

Higher Education Training as a Pipeline for Jobs Creation

It is sad that higher education graduates have to struggle to find their first jobs. How is it possible that those who are trained to create jobs have the hardest of time finding jobs themselves? It should not be that way. I would like to share an anecdote about a similar issue. Once, the ministry of higher education and scientific research happened to visit my university, Alassane Ouattara University in Bouake. Before delivering his speech, the minister wanted to learn about the most urgent challenges the university faced. The first issue that the president of the university raised was the lack of faculty in the College of Law. The ministry was so surprised that he asked, "How do you want me to find faculty members you are supposed to train yourself?"

On the spot, the minister's question went unnoticed, but in hindsight it comes down to the situation of the graduate students who are well-kneaded with knowledge, skills, and experiences but are hardly aware of them. They sit on a treasure they ignore. It is understandable in the sense that rarely do faculty members explore career pathways or prepare their students for careers with their students. Back in the day, this trend is related to the original role of the university. In fact, universities were created to serve two purposes.

> One is as educational establishments and the second as generators of knowledge and technology. As educational establishments, their function is to provide able, self-directed learners that are independent and confident, and will go out into society and give to society through leadership

or through civic duties. As knowledge generators, they are research institutions there to provide new knowledge, to change paradigms, to aid society in its development and in meeting new challenges as they come along.

Along the way, though, the rising of graduate unemployment has drawn heavy criticism about the role of higher education, specifically amid increasing costs. One of the most generally held grudges against the university is that the university does not expose students to real world experience—and what's more the skills taught to the students are obsolete. Whether or not these accusations are legitimate is not the point. Anyway, at some point in time, the university had to react to these accusations by trying to adapt to the changing world. From twofold goals, the university has shifted its theoretical knowledge production focus to a much more practical one, at least partially, extending its role to a four-pronged one, including equipment of graduates for the professional world/

1. Communities dedicated to the learning and personal development of their members, especially students (this could be termed the liberal theory).
2. Sources of expertise and vocational identity (the professional formation theory)
3. Creators, testers, and sites for the evaluation and application of new knowledge (the research engine theory, with an important corollary: the business and industry services theory);
4. Important contributors to society and nations (the civic and community engagement theory)[39]

In a knowledge- and skill-based economy, higher education has acquired the same status as any other productive capital. Along the way, the resonance of universities has increased. Indeed, by their very nature as educational facilities, only universities are able to generate skilled, educated, independent, self-directed individuals capable of bearing value. Geoffrey Boulton summarizes what he perceives as being the role of the university today.

---

[39] Watson et al. (2011), 1–28.

Sources of new knowledge and innovative thinking; providers of skilled personnel and credible credentials; contributors to innovation; attractors of international talent and business investment; agents of social justice and mobility; contributors to social and cultural vitality; and determinants of health and well-being.

In addition, he emphasizes how they contribute to student's success.

They are taught to question interpretations that are given to them, to reduce the chaos of information to the order of an analytical argument and to seek out what is relevant to the resolution of a problem. They learn progressively to identify problems for themselves and to resolve them by rational argument supported by evidence: and they learn not to be dismayed by complexity but to be capable and daring in unravelling it.

Finally, he highlights the outcome of the knowledge and skills that students get at the university not only on their own lives but on the society at large.

When leavened by deep technical understanding, these skills create a powerful alchemy that ensures an annual flux into society of skilled and creative graduates who continually refresh its technical excellence and its economic, social and cultural vitality. They are crucial to its capability to take bold, imaginative and principled action in the face of an uncertain future, rather than cowering in fear of it. They are the qualities that every society needs in its citizens … These are the qualities that ensure that they are not bemused and confounded by the collapse of a world that would have provided them with assured and predictable employment, but make them able, as I say, to be capable and daring in addressing its problems.[40]

The reasoning of Boulton reminds us that there are many education formats, but the university remains the sole place where students can learn to think both critically and creatively. In order to fulfill its new mission, the university had to design the curricula in an integrative manner stretching across disciplines so as to enable students to receive the training in an efficient way. In other words, the university is the only setting where learners can receive an integrative learning enabling them to think on their feet.

How Does Higher Education's Training Pattern Fit into Creative Job Seeking?

In view of this, there is no doubt that universities are living and testing laboratories of theories where projects thrive, thus providing students with a wide array of knowledge, skills, and capabilities, which leads them to think both critically and innovatively in order to play critical roles in their communities.

We all know that major findings stem from universities, but I am not addressing these gigantic projects hosted by universities and whose spinoffs go to the entire university. Rather, I am talking about class and individual projects, dissertations, and research papers. However, as I mentioned earlier, students are hardly aware of this wealth of knowledge that they have acquired in the course of their studies.

With this said, we all know assignments and class projects, and class presentations are pretty common among students. Students work on projects both inside and outside the classroom, as homework or as extra credit work, individually or with a small group, as practice or as hands-on application of the skills they learn in the classroom.

We already underlined the fact that unbeknown to the students, those works contribute to building in them an infinite number of skills, including discipline contents skills, information management skills, and people skills.

---

[40] Geoffrey Boulton, "Global: What Are Universities For?" *University World News*, The Global Windows on Higher Education, March 2009.

Nevertheless, above and beyond these immediate benefits, these classes and extracurricular works can alleviate people's pain, because their main characteristic is that they are always an innovative approach to a common problem.[41]

Thus, these projects can contribute to creating opportunities for the students themselves in a morose environment undermined by unemployment. Some of these projects may need to be slightly revamped, but they are still valid and hold the core elements as development projects.

Another way to get a head start is to make one's dissertation (either master's or doctorate) work one's way through the job. It is a question of obtaining the research topic from an institution or company. One big misconception that students preparing a doctorate hold is thinking that a doctorate is made solely for teaching at the university. Organizations, institutions, and companies also need doctors to push their research and development agendas. Being able to work on various aspects of the same topic at various academic levels under the supervision of an institution or a company gives the candidate an extensive experience and places him in the ideal spot to be hired at a later time by the institution or company in question. Such situations are common with development institutions and not-for-profit organizations whose work is essentially project based. Through collaborations and partnerships, the university can also spearhead this scheme to help its graduates secure their first professional assignments. Undoubtedly, a master's or doctorate student who has been working on a topic for a number of years in collaboration with an institution or organization can rely on enough connections and gathered enough experience to be considered for a full-time contract. In the worst-case scenario, he may end up as a consultant.

Start One's Own Small Business

Being able to give life to that entrepreneurial idea that has been brewing in the back of the head is an opportunity to create value. The graduate student does not always need to reach out to others for an employment. He can be his own boss.

---

[41] Typically, a business is meant to address and solve a specific problem.

Indeed, after graduating, students can opt to set up their own small businesses. Those who want to make money fast should opt for creating their own enterprise because company or government jobs will never make them wealthy.

However, the news about the lifetime of small businesses is far from reassuring. Some sources argue that 90 percent of small businesses and start-ups alike are doomed to fail before their fifth anniversaries. I will not cover start-ups here because a small business is different from a start-up. A start-up is mostly if not entirely technology focused, and as a consequence it is bound to growth fast due to the market it is targeting. The term itself and the image it conveys originate in the technological hustle and bustle in the early 1990s with the generalization of the internet. With this being said, here is what the Small Business Association has to say about start-ups: "The term startup is also associated with a business that is typically technology oriented and has high growth potential, and a massive original capital, which a traditional small business cannot afford."

Conversely, a small business venture starts at a relatively small scale due to the fact that the initial investment comes mostly from loans and grants. What is interesting about small businesses is that they do not necessarily need a high initial investment to operate, which spurs the question: "What does it really takes to start a small business?"

This question warrants consideration at a time when everybody is trying to set up a business with funding; generally it's massive funding. As an educator and students' mentor and coach, I had various interesting conversations with my students about the issue. Whenever I ask them why they do not start their own businesses if finding jobs has been the most difficult thing they have to face, the reply is almost always, "I need the money." Then I ask them where the money is supposed to come from. Unfortunately, my students are the only ones to think that starting a small business equates big funding. I used to go on to tell them that it would be hard to get the funding, particularly because most of their projects necessitate well over US$1,000.[42] On the other hand, I tell them that no bank will trust them due to their lack of experience and assets. Finally, they

---

[42] In some countries, this starting capital might sound like peanuts, but in Africa it is a lot of money in a poverty-stricken context, particularly when only one member of the family has to support the entire family.

stand at the point where no family member can entrust them with such an amount of money, and neither will any financial institution, including microfinance.

Actually, one of the reasons why a business fails, generally speaking, is the lack of experience of the entrepreneur. On this basis, I used to tell my students that if people happen to loan them this money, they have done them a disservice. Their lack of practical experience in the field would make them vulnerable and then expose them to failure.

Suppose a family member lends them this money to start this business after multiple pleas. It is great to have the support of one's family, but the lack of experience is a big impediment for the success of this business. In addition to that, one of the reasons why I do not give much for such businesses is the moral hazard to which they are subject. Because students want their projects to look and sound viable, most of them lay out the business plans without budgeting all the miscellaneous expenses that they make incur. For instance, no expenditure item would mention the rent or the allowance, although it is important when starting off in life. That is because as soon as they launch the business, they are likely to run out of cash shortly afterward. This might result in tension in the family and lay the ground for resentment. That is why I always advise them to start off with what they have, because a business is an idea and the vision associated with this idea.

The Online Business Dictionary describes the vision as "An inspirational description of what an organization would like to achieve or accomplish in the mid-term or long-term future. It is intended to serve as a clear guide for choosing current and future courses of action."[43]

Why is the vision crucial to the small business starter? According to Jesse Lyn Stoner, a vision has three main dimensions: purpose, picture of the future, and values.

The purpose is why the business has been created in the first place. Having a sense of purpose is extremely important. Most people hold the misconception that only a small number of smart people are capable of coming up with a brilliant idea that will carry great value to their community. Nothing could be further from the truth. Let us recall that a business idea stems from a lack of something. It is mainly about decrypting

---

[43] http://www.businessdictionary.com/definition/vision-statement.html.

the shortcomings of its immediate environment. There are numerous needs that are unmet, even though there are others that need to be created. But let us focus on the unmet needs. All we need to do is to look around us and use our critical and imaginative minds. Therefore one can argue with confidence that for students, there has never been a better time for them to start their own small businesses.

The second dimension is picture of the future. It is not enough to have the great idea and then be wiped out of the landscape. It is not like "shining under the intense spotlight like a precious meteorite fallen down from the sky," It is all about how growth and expansion are envisioned altogether. Everybody is not going to turn out like Bill Gates or Steve Jobs, but it is fundamentally about making an enduring impact. At this point, it is important to draw a difference between an entrepreneur and an owner of a small business who strives to live from hand to mouth because he has no plan for the future. I dare say that such businesses will never experience growth—and worse, they will whittle away and go bankrupt. Once again, vision and clarity in terms of scaling need to go hand in hand. Thus as a clear answer to the initial question, I would say that the smallest is the best because not only can the business be self-funded, but the more it grows, the more the entrepreneur gains experience and proves his worth.

Yet there is a number of commitments that need to be put in place to support the vision before it becomes reality; if not, it would remain more a form of wishful thinking than a reality. For example, how many hours the entrepreneur is determined to put in and how tight the budget he is willing to live on (at least during the first five years till the business takes root) will make all the difference.

I am still convinced that the students already possess numerous technical knowledge and skills that can enable them to be successful in everything they set their heart on.

Figure 1: The Entrepreneurship Triangle

https://seapointcenter.com/what-is-vision.

Turning Problems into Solutions: Watching Trends and the Consultant Mind-Set

The assumption that they are being trained for existing jobs, or at least that the government will be helping them secure their first employment, is pretty common among students despite the numerous challenges the public authorities have been facing over the last two decades. In some countries, efforts have been made to promote and support small businesses, but in others the official bodies have never have the courage to tell graduates that they have run out of steam and are unable to provide jobs to each and every student exiting universities. I had numerous occasions to discuss with my students that jobs are not ready for them after they graduate.

Still, they are confronted with the harsh reality when, several years after they complete their diplomas, they are unable to get even their first job, and that they are compelled to accept a small job that has nothing to do with what they were trained for. It is not that the graduates do not have the necessary skills to hold a position. Not at all. Moreover, many experts in the workforce development field are targeting companies' human resources—gatekeepers who failed to see the big picture about applicants instead of being solely focused on a piece of paper called a résumé or curriculum vitae.

Yet that will not happen by itself. Then there is a need for a paradigm shift.[44] In other words, the students need to alter their usual way of thinking about joining the workforce after college. Instead of banking on the idea that a job has been waiting for them (so they need to get the skills necessary to execute the job), they should think of creative ways to add value to the activities of those who may need their expertise.

I understand the fact that students having certain backgrounds like medicine, law, or engineering are privileged compared to those who are in the humanities or liberal arts in the way that the former are trained for specific purposes whereas the latter are trained for general purposes. As a result, medical and engineer students have to go through a practicum period as part of their regular training pattern, which gives them a leg up on the work market because of the experience they have been accumulating during their training. Conversely, no internship, externship, or placement scheme is required for students stemming from the humanities and liberal arts, which in same way places them at risk of not getting any experience by the time they graduate. Then what happens to them? This is where students can sell their expertise to companies. And for those with a general background, I would recommend they get involved in community service projects as a way to gather experience and transferable skills they may apply in many other sectors, particularly in the broad development field; it may help them find their job pathway. With a bit of luck, it can also be conducive to a job.

My personal experience in Germany is compelling. From 1998 to 2002, I was in Germany because I wanted to complete my graduate studies as part of adding international experience to my résumé. I could not do it because it was impossible to transition from a visitor status to a student one. To cut a long story short, I abandoned this project and took to flexing both the German and English languages, along with other subject matters. In the meantime, I was engaged in a legal procedure to extend my stay in this country. After taking the European Language Test in Germany and the

---

[44] Coined by the American philosopher Thomas Kuhn (1922-1996), the term "paradigm shift" literally means a change in the theoretical framework or the underlying assumption. The concept is extensively exploited in his seminal work, *The Structure of Scientific Revolutions*, published in 1962.

British Chamber of Commerce Exam in commercial and industrial English, I decided to volunteer my time because I did not know when I would be departing from the country. I went to the town hall to meet up with my counselor and asked him whether he knew organizations where I could volunteer my time. He gave me the name of two organizations right away, AWO and SCI. With AWO, the use of the computer was not widespread like today, so my role was to initiate a group of midterm professionals to the basics of Microsoft Office. In the case of SCI, a community and learning center for dropout youth, I was tasked to instruct language skills to two young Turkish who had just arrived in Germany. I do not want to go into all the details, but after two months, the director called me in his office and asked me how I'd managed to develop those speaking skills in the two youth; they had confidence and were able to have basic conversations with their German peers. I explained him how I'd proceeded. Then he thanked me wholeheartedly and took the opportunity to extend an invitation to me for the year-end picnic celebration somewhere in a remote woods. It was in July 2001, and I believed that it would be the last I would see him. I was wrong because in September, he called me in his office and asked me to go to the Ministry of Labor for a work permit because he was offering the position of computer instructor in his center.

Unfortunately, I could not secure that permit because the procedure for my returning to my country had already been completed and a date had been set; I had to go back. I was a bit disappointed because I would have liked to get that job and stay in Germany for good. What I would like to point out here is how relevant and crucial volunteering commitment and selflessness can pave the way for a full-time commitment.

Otherwise, graduate students whose curricula draw on research can turn companies' problems into solutions by watching the news and following trends. I already mentioned in the beginning of this part that in an ever-changing and competitive world, companies are constantly solving both internal and external problems to stay in the game. Every day they make the headlines, either rising or falling. Happily, company reports are readily made available online, and there are specialized newspapers. Coupled with that is the ability to keep abreast of the labor market information and interpret it as an asset.

On the other hand, no matter how well a company is doing, it will not scoff the prospect of making more money because it's hard to imagine a company that will not fulfill its primary purpose. Remember the old saying "The more you eat, the bigger your appetite"? If this saying is true for healthy companies, it is all even truer for companies having trouble. The most interesting about the whole thing is that more than ever, companies have been on the lookout to hire talented people to solve their most pressing problems. Therefore I dare say that never has the times been better for students to strut their stuff. The university gives them what it takes to constantly look for new ways to solve old problems like big players, through creativity and innovation. Henry Kaiser, an American industrialist, said that problems are only opportunities in work clothes. In other words, it is envisioning oneself in the company and formulating a strategy that will take it to new heights. I feel like saying the particular skill set needed here is problem solving, but in reality it is time to convene both hard and soft skill sets accumulated in the course of one's studies. They're pretty much like job seekers, because the end result of proposing solutions to companies is to be hired to implement these solutions. In this case, the problem-solving pattern with a specific focus on productivity and profitability through processes improvement or sales boost proves more than relevant.

Internships, Externships, and Placement Opportunities as Stepping-Stones to a Job Offer

I mentioned earlier that internship and externship, in addition to being résumé experiences, provide students with an excellent opportunity to build up significant professional experience. In addition to that, they are a fertile ground for networking. It is my understanding that some students from specific colleges may be entitled to a compulsory internship or externship as part of their academic endeavors. For those who do not necessarily need it to graduate, I would recommend them finding one. It does not mean that an internship or externship will end up in a job offer, but it might also be a matter of time before your efforts are rewarded, especially if you do a good job.

Deep down, I believe that the return on investment of any form of prior professional involvement is countless and even underestimated. In fact, there is much more to the internship, externship, or placement than meets the eyes. They can be more than just helping students acquire knowledge related to a specific field or industry. Rather, they can be a foolproof way for students to access or create job opportunities for themselves. One fact about these professional involvements is that they give college students experiential learning opportunities by applying classroom concepts to an actual work environment, so as to get a preview of what day-to-day activities look like. Another advantage is that the intern or extern is part of the company's team, performing real tasks, working against deadlines, and getting firsthand knowledge and hands-on experience just like a regular employee. In some cases, they may shadow their supervisors, and in most cases they are tasked with a set of activities to complete in a certain amount of time. Most internships and externships are rarely paid positions, but as an analyst put forward, "The emphasis is on learning, so the real payback is in gaining experience outside the academic environment. That experience, in turn, can be valuable resume content, especially for students with little or no internship experience. The tradeoff of experience will typically have a positive payback even if the financial payout is minimal."

An internship or an externship is a unique opportunity to see and experience the actual equipment and practical techniques used by professionals. This is what an expert says about medical extern:

> During a typical externship, the medical assistant may be required to complete several tasks. These often include such things as job shadowing, attending conferences, learning a variety of medical topics, and counseling. A well-designed externship program will allow the extern to be involved in staff meetings and company development opportunities, allowing the medical assistant to view and be involved in every aspect of the business operations. In fact, these are invaluable occasions, That can give you an invaluable insider's view of the realities of a company or profession to help you decide if it's a direction you really want to pursue … In short, think of an externship as a

quick and easy way for you to gain information about your intended career … And more than that, an internship or externship can be a stepping stone to a full-time job.

My point here is that because an intern or extern is exposed to the challenges of a daily job, he can use this prominent position to uncover opportunities, just like in the previous section. The difference is that in this case, he is acting as an insider and not an outsider, which gives him enough space and confidence to ask working professionals questions that he would have never been able to do if he had not been there.

As a result, like a researcher, he may collect all the relevant data that would allow him to set up a strategic plan that could help the company or the structure improve processes or productivity, save money, or make more money.[45]

At any event, if the college student wants to draft a "rescue package" as an outsider or an insider, the main tool that he needs is analytics.

According to the online dictionary Techopedia, "Analytics is the scientific process of discovering and communicating the meaningful patterns which can be found in data. It is concerned with turning raw data into insight for making better decisions. Analytics relies on the application of statistics, computer programming, and operations research in order to quantify and gain insight to the meanings of data. It is especially useful in areas which record a lot of data or information."[46] Analytics prove efficient principally because they involve "studying past historical data to research potential trends, to analyze the effects of certain decisions or events, or to evaluate the performance of a given tool or scenario. The goal of analytics is to improve the business by gaining knowledge which can be used to make improvements or changes."

In a broader sense, though, analytics may refer to any research procedure or methodology consisting in pitching business ideas and developing

---

[45] Regardless of the number of responsibilities and the number of daily working hours that you might have as an intern or extern, you need to "treat the experience as if you were heading out each day to a job. Show up on time, be professional, be focused and engaged all day every day. Remember that you're there to learn, so be respectful, ask questions and be the best that you can be."

[46] https://www.techopedia.com/definition/30296/analytics.

solutions through a problem-solving perspective to existing organizations. In other words, the focus is the identification of the gaps and development and proposal of action plans. Roughly speaking, the problem-solving steps are as follows: defining the problem, identifying the behaviors that needs to change, analyzing the root causes of the problem, collecting data, finding the best methodology and the right tools to analyze them, drawing conclusions, and making significant recommendations. For those involved with invention, they may follow the same pattern to develop innovative solutions to an existing problem and create a low-fidelity prototype.

Once again, the technical skills and competencies are the essential part of this process, but the soft skills should not be neglected, because they are the ones that help you put your best self on show once you get the chance to present your product to the audience. Here is a summary of an example related by Dale Carnegie in *How to Win Friends and Influence People* of how one of his auditors used this strategy to secure a job with one of the most inaccessible employers in the region by coming to see that difficult man with a sound and relevant business project.[47]

The Surefire Strategy to Be Approved as an Outsider: Finding an Inside Ally

The example is extracted from the time-honored book *How to Win Friends and Influence People*. The protagonist did not go to the finicky boss empty-handed. Before even thinking of stepping out for the job, he learned his lesson. He understood that in the interaction between employer and prospective employee, because of the imbalance of power, he thought out his bargaining chip by masterminding a sound proposal and brought it to the negotiation table. And he won the battle.

However, though this *extrapreneurship* approach of crafting a project from scratch for a company or organization might pass up as a single example of its kind in the sense that the context today is different in light of the high number of competitors, it may be best to involve an inside

---

[47] Dale Carnegie, *How to Win Friends and Influence People* (Cornerstone Publishing, 2005), 99–100.

man at a very early stage of the project design.[48] It is important and even vital to call for input from an undercover agent because it will help the project owner gain unique insights into data accuracy and procedures from an internal perspective and, for the counterpart, foster inclusion and participation in the decision-making process. As a result, the internal ally feels a sense of value, appreciation, and recognition, which leads to a sense of ownership and ultimately eases the acceptance and buy-in of the project by the management team.

In psychology, ownership means possession. It implies three elements: efficacy, or the ability to generate a preferred or intended outcome; self-identity as an emblematic representation of the self; and a sense of belonging or possession illustrated by the IKEA effect as the increase in valuation of self-made products.[49] Similarly, making way for the inside man to have a say in the project planning in a collaborative manner will give rise to his motivation, loyalty, accountability, and responsibility. In essence, this approach is part of building a productive relationship.

The Elevator Pitch

I would like to say one word about the elevator pitch.[50] Alternatively called elevator speech, the elevator pitch is a quick synopsis of your background and experience. It is so called because it should be able to be delivered quickly when in an elevator. Essentially, the elevator pitch is who you are, what you do, and what you want to do as a job hunter, and as such it should be thirty to sixty seconds. It is a tool that can be used in job interviews as an answer to the tricky prompt "Tell me about yourself."

A lot of career advisers and career counselors see it as a powerful marketing and networking tool, so they recommend drafting and rehearsing till you are able to deliver it in a natural way before even thinking to apply to any job. Before you set foot into any type of professional networking

---

[48] The word *extrapreneurship* is my own creation.

[49] Michael I. Norton, Daniel Norton, and Dan Ariely, "The IKEA Effect: When Labor Leads to Love," *Journal of Consumer Psychology* 22, no. 3 (July 2012): 453–60.

[50] I purposefully talked about the elevator pitch near the end for one reason: it can serve all the job-search occurrences described in this book.

event, you should have your elevator pitch down pat. Know what you do, how to talk about it, and—well—how to make yourself sound good. Once you have this ready, practice it a few times in front of the mirror. You'll feel much more confident come the time of the professional networking event.

As good as an elevator pitch can be, I think job seekers do not have to worry much about finding the perfect elevator pitch because it is built in the career preparation process. Indeed, as the French author Nicolas Boileau once said, "Whatever is well conceived is clearly said, And the words to say it flow with ease."

I say this because all the way though the preparation process, the applicant learns the jargon of the industry he or she has been interested in so that he or she appears as a specialist in the field. Therefore, as soon the applicant is given the chance to demonstrate what he or she can practically bring to the table, he or she can swiftly and persuasively ignite the interest of the listener.

In addition to that, the elevator speech is a good means of introducing the qualifications, skills, unique selling points, and special value of the consultant who wants to sell his or her services to companies via a solution package.

Takeaways

On the rocky road of the job search process, graduates need to know that through the intracurriculum and extracurriculum integration and cocurricular teachings embedded in curricula and class-based activities and projects, they have the necessary skills and competencies to succeed in their future careers regardless of the type of activities in which they want to engage.

To add to that, internships, externships, and placements, even though they are primarily meant to help students acquire day-to-day professional experience through the development of skills valuable in the workplace, represent invaluable job opportunities because they can be a springboard for students to make meaningful and relevant proposals aiming at solving organizational problems, and thus they are ways and means to create job opportunities that put students' feet into the workforce door.

CONCLUDING NOTES

The job-search journey for the graduated student is nothing if not lengthy, rocky, and dragging, involving a lot of planning, thinking, decision-making, and determination. In a fast-paced and technology-driven world, the job market has never been in such turmoil, and this trend is probably set to continue and increase.

On the other hand, the university is better than any other training institution that provides the students with the best tools to succeed in life. The reason why the number of students enrolled in higher education increases every year might be attributed to that factor, let alone that universities remain economic and cultural powerhouses. Based on studies, universities like University of Chicago and Pennsylvania State contribute US$6.7 billion and US$11.6 billion, respectively, to the economies of their states, which reminds us that the so-called higher education inefficiency certainly originates in a huge miscommunication between trainers and trainees, university leadership, faculty, and students.

On one side, university administrators are more preoccupied by means and ways of attracting and retaining the maximum number of students in order to maintain their reputation—without necessary complying with the basics: student success.

On the other side, faculty are concerned only with the quality of the narrow content of their teaching, and thus they have neglected to introduce students to ways to translate this technical knowledge into practical skill sets usable in a job setting.

Finally, more often than not, the students make poor choices about their future careers. As a consequence of all that, the students are the ones who generally fall through the cracks.

Nonetheless, the university remains a powerful institution of higher learning where students acquire the weapons to face the challenges of the outside world.

In fact, with early preparation, college students can still make a painless transition from new grads to new hires because higher education equips them with the right methods and tools to blaze their own paths and ultimately recapture control of their own lives. A survey conducted in 2017 by the National Association of Colleges and Employers (NACE) in the Job Outlook 2018 revealed that the top two skill sets that employers value the most in the workplace are critical thinking and problem solving. Those skill sets are immediately followed by teamwork, professionalism, and work ethic as foundational skills relevant to the professional world.

For what this research is worth, I can state with confidence that in the coursework alone, students are exposed to a wide variety of skills, including those cited above—not to mention the class assignments, presentations, and projects. As an employer said, problem solving is more important than a college major. He is perfectly right from his own perspective, as all the skill sets mentioned as necessary in the workforce are already at play among students. They simply need to open their eyes.

On the other side, given those skills combined with the proven fact that innovation is what keeps companies competitive and growing, never in history are students well put to take full control of their lives and create sustainable, independent lives for themselves during or after their studies.

Bearing this in mind—that there are numerous ways in which the graduate student can easily find a job or contribute to creating job opportunities—the spectrum goes from volunteering or community service to internship, externship, and placement.

However, seeking a job is nothing like making an appointment to see the doctor or go grocery shopping. All the described processes may not happen overnight. On the contrary, it may take a while before the graduated student lands a dream job, but hopefully with a pinch of patience and a hint of faith, the student will triumph in this jungle.

In short, by being active, proactive, and intentional about one's professional development and career, one can have entire control of one's future career and be the ideal person every company or organization will be seeking.

Printed in the United States
By Bookmasters